O9-AHW-353

Good Food Made Simple

VEGETARIAN

Good Food Made Simple

VEGETARIAN

*Over 140 delicious recipes, 500 color photographs,
step-by-step images, and nutritional information*

This edition published in 2013
LOVE FOOD is an imprint of Parragon Books Ltd

Parragon Inc.
440 Park Avenue South, 13th Floor
New York, NY 10016

www.parragon.com/lovefood

ISBN: 978-1-4723-1919-7

Printed in China

Additional design by Geoff Borin
New photography by Noel Murphy
New home economy by Sue Henderson
New recipes by Teresa Goldfinch
Introduction and notes by Sarah Bush
Edited by Fiona Biggs
Nutritional analysis by Fiona Hunter

Notes for the Reader
This book uses standard kitchen measuring spoons and cups. All spoon and cup
measurements are level unless otherwise indicated. Unless otherwise stated,
milk is assumed to be whole, eggs are large, individual vegetables are medium,
and pepper is freshly ground black pepper. Unless otherwise stated, all root
vegetables should be washed and peeled before using.

Garnishes, decorations and serving suggestions are all optional and not
necessarily included in the recipe ingredients or method. Any optional
ingredients and seasoning to taste are not included in the nutritional analysis.
The times given are an approximate guide only. Preparation times may differ
according to the techniques used by different people and the cooking times
may also vary from those given. Optional ingredients, variations or serving
suggestions have not been included in the time calculations.

Recipes using raw or very lightly cooked eggs should be avoided by infants, the
elderly, pregnant women, and people with weakened immune systems. Pregnant
and breast-feeding women are advised to avoid eating peanuts and peanut
products. People with nut allergies should be aware that some of the prepared
ingredients used in the recipes in this book may contain nuts. Always check the
packaging before use.

The publisher has taken great care to select ingredients for the recipes used
in this book that are suitable for those following a vegetarian diet. Always read
labels carefully and, if necessary, check with the manufacturer before use.

Contents

Vegetarian cooking

There are many misconceptions surrounding a vegetarian diet but, put simply, someone following this program removes meat, fish, and poultry from their meals and replaces them with vegetables, grains, pasta, beans, fresh fruit, and nuts. Today, more and more people are considering replacing two or three dinners a week with a vegetarian alternative—while others may have decided to convert completely.

Equally, almost all of us will know someone within our family circle or friends who is a vegetarian, so it is important to understand the basic principles when cooking for them.

Benefits of a vegetarian diet

You may be surprised, but the Western diet used to consist mainly of cereals, beans, and vegetables because most people grew their own food or bought it locally, and meat or poultry was considered a luxury only for special occasions. This high fiber, low-fat, low-sugar, low-salt diet was far healthier for us, and illnesses that are common today were rare. The availability of mass-produced processed foods has made our lives easier, but has created more of a concern for our health.

New inspirations

Today, being vegetarian is much easier than it was in the past. For a start, there are many more ingredients available in our supermarkets, health-food stores, and ethnic food stores. Many other cultures, whose diets tend to revolve more around vegetables, are increasingly influencing our diets, and we can draw on spicy seasonings from Asia, robust flavors from the Mediterranean, and exciting grain dishes from Africa. Traveling to vacation destinations farther afield has encouraged people to sample the unfamiliar and increased a desire to cook similar dishes back home. Restaurants are more aware of the changing trends of eating and include meatless choices on their menus, which are enjoyed by vegetarians and nonvegetarians alike.

Explore your local ethnic food stores to find a range of exciting ingredients and spices.

Vegetarians and the environment

The range of fresh produce today is increasing, with growers and producers tempting us with new foods. Growing our own vegetables, fruit, and herbs is more popular and farmer's markets spring up regularly in towns all over the country. By shopping locally, we support small businesses and help lessen our environmental impact. A supply of fresh, organically grown vegetables, fruit, and salads are just on our doorstep—a boon to the vegetarian diet. Sometimes you pay a premium for this because harvesting is done on a smaller scale, often by hand, instead of using large-scale machinery; however, if you're not buying expensive meat and poultry items each week, you'll be spending less.

Vegetarians and vegans

When considering the pros and cons of changing your eating habits, you should investigate the various approaches to vegetarian food. Some people consider themselves vegetarian yet they eat fish, and others will eat chicken. Then there are those who follow a vegan diet and only eat foods of plant origin and, therefore, don't eat milk, butter, eggs, or even honey. Whichever route you choose, variety is the key to maintaining a balanced diet.

The recipes included in this book do not include any meat or fish products, but may contain dairy, such as eggs, milk, and cheese, so are not suitable for vegans, unless specified.

Maintaining a balanced diet

The vegetarian diet is not complicated or as time-consuming as it is sometimes thought. Likewise, it's not automatically healthy and requires a combination of different ingredients to achieve the right balance. Don't be overly worried about this aspect; just be aware of what your body needs to work efficiently and make sure you include those things in your diet.

Proteins

These are essential for healthy growth and repair of cells as well as protection against infection and building up resistance. The daily requirement for the body is small and there is no problem getting enough as long as you are following a varied vegetarian diet. The main sources are:

• Dairy—eggs, cheese, yogurt, and milk.

• Cereals— rice, oats, corn, wheat and flour products, pasta, couscous, barley, and rye.

• Legumes—dried beans, including soy products (such as tofu), chickpeas, and lentils.

• Seeds and nuts—walnuts, brazil nuts, pecans, almonds, cashew nuts, pine nuts, peanuts and peanut butter, pumpkin seeds, sunflower seeds, flax seeds, sesame seeds, and tahini paste.

Carbohydrates

The body needs carbohydrates for energy, and they are found in starches and natural sugar. The easiest way to consume them is in the form of grains, so foods using flour to make bread, cakes, and cookies should be included in the diet. Both pasta and potatoes are a good source, too.

It's difficult to eat too many carbohydrates because they are the "filler" ingredients that we eat at most meals. They are not responsible for weight gain, as is often thought; weight gain tends to be due to the excessive amounts of fat eaten with them.

Sugar

Refined sugar is an energy food and measured amounts found in jellies, preserves, and honey is the most straightforward way to include it in the diet. Too many of these calories, however, and the body will be unable to burn off the excess and they will be stored as body fat. It is better to enjoy natural sugars packed into fresh fruit, which come with the added bonus of fiber and will fill you more quickly.

Fats

History shows us that fats and oils have been an essential ingredient in the human diet for centuries, and they come from two sources—plants and animals. The only animal fat included in the vegetarian diet is that found in eggs, and in milk and other dairy products made from it, such as cream, butter, and cheese.

Other fats regularly used come from plants, either in the form of oils or spreads and hard vegetable fats, such as margarine. There are many issues regarding the intake of fats, whether they are saturated (solid animal fats), unsaturated (olive oil), or polyunsaturated (vegetable oils), with many different opinions.

The healthiest is generally considered to be unsaturated fat, and in some countries, such as those around the Mediterranean, where this form of fat is included in the diet, they appear to have a lower incidence of heart disease.

Another consideration is that butter, which is a natural product, is preferable to using margarines and some oils that have been heavily processed. Whichever path you choose to take, it is generally accepted that a reduced intake of fat is the healthiest option.

Other essentials

To make sure a vegetarian diet is balanced and includes all the elements your body requires, you need to follow certain principles. Once you have become familiar with the best foods to eat in the right quantities, everything else will fall into place. Plan your meals to include reasonable portions of grains and food made from them with plenty of fruit and vegetables. Eat moderate amounts of dairy, eggs, peas, beans, lentils, and nuts, and small portions of fats, sugar, tea, coffee, and alcohol.

All these foods form part of a balanced diet, so it shouldn't be necessary to take vitamin supplements, unless prescribed by your doctor.

Vitamins & minerals

While concentrating on other aspects of the vegetarian diet, sometimes the essential nutrients in the form of vitamins and minerals can be forgotten.

The body needs vitamins from the B group, iron, and zinc to help process foods and allow for the nervous system to function properly. They can be found in:

- whole-grain cereals
- breads and pasta
- nuts and seeds
- dried beans
- potatoes
- fresh and dried fruit
- leafy green vegetables
- soy products
- yeast extract.

Combining foods

One other point to consider in the vegetarian diet is that by excluding certain foods that come from animal sources (meat, poultry, and fish) you are excluding proteins that are known as "complete." When digested, these are used by the body to make essential proteins of its own.

Although cheese and eggs are also "complete," they can only be eaten by vegetarians in moderate quantities to avoid a fat overload and vegans do not have this option at all. It's necessary to combine complementary proteins either in one meal or within a few hours. This is not as difficult as it may seem and you probably do it already—just think hummus and pita bread, pasta and cheese, granola with nuts and seeds, and rice and bean dishes.

Sourcing & substituting

Changing set eating habits will not happen overnight, so don't worry if at first your menus aren't perfectly balanced. Each day will take you a step closer to your chosen way of eating as you buy different ingredients and try out new recipes. Shop regularly for fresh vegetables and include them in as many meals as possible. Gradually change to whole-food products instead of the processed ones, choose reduced-fat versions of foods you usually buy, and look more closely at lists of ingredients on packages to avoid high fat, salt, or additives.

Hidden animal products

Animal products may be included in many prepared foods.

For example:

- pastry may contain animal suet or lard

- cheese is often made with animal rennet as a coagulator

- candies and desserts may include gelatin that comes from an animal source

- manufactured cakes will have eggs and dairy in them

- many bottled sauces contain anchovies

- wine can be made using animal products in the fining process.

Start reading the small print on food labels to check what's included.

Finding out more

If you are searching for more detailed information about what is contained in prepared products, reputable sites on the Internet offer a wealth of easily accessible information and advice.

Pantry essentials

Start to build up a pantry of useful ingredients, including dried beans and whole-wheat pasta. Keep a stock of different varieties of canned beans for quick meals, when you don't have time to soak them in advance. Have a selection of olive, seed, and flavored oils, dried spices, and seasonings for the new recipes you will be discovering.

Freezing

Your freezer will be a good friend. Take the time to cook double quantities of recipes, so you can pack half of it into containers to be used at a later date. There are hints about freezing many of the recipes in this book.

The everyday vegetarian

When you start out on the road to total or part-time vegetarianism, meal planning will be the first step. Your own favorite recipes will make a good starting point by just replacing certain ingredients.

Some simple changes

• Make a spaghetti sauce with lentils replacing the meat (see page 174).

• A spicy Bean & Vegetable Chili (see page 188) is a great alternative to a meat-based one.

• You can make homemade soups (see pages 68-88) with vegetable stock and by using grains or beans to thicken.

• Bean Burgers (see page 202) will be winners with children.

• There's a huge range of delicious vegetarian toppings for pizza, including some more unusual sweet ones (see page 260).

Vegetarians and meat eaters

If you are catering for both vegetarians and nonvegetarians, it doesn't have to be difficult—you just need to think a little about the menus and plan a few changes. Try to create menus that everyone can eat instead of cooking separate dishes. As long as a meal is balanced and varied, most people will be happy to eat vegetarian dishes—and may not even notice!

A vegetarian diet for children

When considering a vegetarian diet for children, exactly the same principles apply. Careful monitoring of their diet, making sure they are not missing out on essential foods, will insure that they are healthy, energetic, and growing at the correct rate.

Few parents are able to raise children without worries and concerns over their eating patterns, but just be sure to include plenty of high-vitality foods that are as fresh and unprocessed as possible. Always have wholesome snacks available:

- precut fresh fruit
- small helpings of dried apricots, raisins, and cranberries
- vegetable sticks
- rice cakes
- cheese cubes
- yogurts.

Offer water or diluted fruit juice instead of sweet soft drinks. You could also make your own ice pops using fruit puree with little or no added sugar.

Involving children in helping to prepare and cook meals will encourage them to try new foods.

Above all, don't be scared off. Moving either completely, or partly, toward a vegetarian diet is not difficult. It will open the door to a tasty and healthy new approach to food and cooking that you and your friends and family will love.

Apple & Seed Muesli *18*

Oatmeal Crunch *20*

Honey & Rosemary Roasted Plums *22*

Oatmeal with Fruit & Nuts *24*

Fresh Croissants *26*

Strawberry Cream Cheese Spread *28*

Eggs Florentine *30*

Muesli Pancake Stack with Honey *32*

French Toast Waffles *34*

Pancake Eggs Benedict *36*

Pancakes with Baked Mushrooms *38*

Mushroom Bruschetta *40*

Roasted Bell Pepper Ciabatta with Chopped Eggs & Olives *42*

Croissants with Berries & Mascarpone *44*

Zucchini Fritters with Eggs & Caramelized Onions *46*

Asparagus & Egg Pastries *48*

Cinnamon Swirls *50*

Apple Danish *52*

Yogurt with Blueberries, Honey & Nuts *54*

Muesli Muffins *56*

Grilled Mozzarella Eggplant Bagels *58*

Celery & Apple Smoothie *60*

Red Pepper Smoothie *62*

Apricot Smoothie *64*

Breakfast & Brunch

Apple & Seed Muesli

 SERVES 10   PREP TIME: 15 minutes plus cooling   COOKING TIME: 4 minutes

nutritional information per serving	325 cal, 12g fat, 1g sat fat, 16g total sugars, trace salt

Nutty and fruity, this is a great healthy start to the day. Serve with milk or mix with yogurt.

INGREDIENTS

½ cup sunflower seeds

¼ cup pumpkin seeds

¾ cup coarsely chopped, shelled hazelnuts

2½ cups buckwheat flakes

2½ cups rice flakes

3 cups millet flakes

1⅓ cups coarsely chopped dried apple

¾ cup coarsely chopped, dried pitted dates

1. Heat a nonstick skillet over medium heat. Add the seeds and hazelnuts and lightly toast, shaking the skillet frequently, for 4 minutes, or until golden brown. Transfer to a large bowl and let cool.

2. Add the flakes, apple, and dates to the bowl and mix thoroughly until combined. Store the muesli in an airtight jar or container.

SOMETHING
DIFFERENT
For extra
sweetness and
crunch, try
topping with
slices of fresh
apple or pear.

Oatmeal Crunch

 SERVES 2

PREP TIME:
10 minutes

COOKING TIME:
8 minutes

nutritional information per serving	362 cal, 17g fat, 2g sat fat, 7g total sugars, 0.5g salt

Make oatmeal more exciting with the addition of plump apricots, almonds, and sunflower seeds. A great breakfast choice on chilly days.

INGREDIENTS

1 cup rolled oats

2 cups water

small pinch of salt

2 tablespoons chopped dried apricots

2 tablespoons toasted slivered almonds

4 teaspoons sunflower seeds

1. Mix the oats with the water and salt in a nonstick saucepan and stir well. Bring to a boil over medium–high heat, stirring occasionally, then reduce the heat and simmer, continuing to stir occasionally, for 5 minutes.

2. When the oatmeal is thick and creamy, spoon into two serving bowls and top with the apricots, almonds, and sunflower seeds. Serve immediately.

HEALTHY HINT
If you prefer
a creamier cereal,
use half low-fat
milk and half
water.

Honey & Rosemary Roasted Plums

SERVES 4

PREP TIME:
15 minutes
plus cooling

COOKING TIME:
25–35 minutes

nutritional information
per serving   316 cal, 18g fat, 11g sat fat, 27g total sugars, 0.2g salt

These plums look pretty bathed in their ruby syrup.

INGREDIENTS

4 firm, ripe red plums
3–4 fresh rosemary sprigs
⅓ cup honey
finely grated zest and juice of
½ orange
½ cup heavy cream
⅔ cup Greek-style yogurt
¾ cup muesli

1. Preheat the oven to 375°F. Halve and pit the plums, then arrange them cut side up in an ovenproof dish large enough to hold them in a single layer. Bruise the rosemary sprigs with a rolling pin and push them among the fruit.

2. Mix together the honey, orange juice, and orange zest, then pour the mixture over the top of the plums. Cover the dish with aluminum foil and bake for 25–35 minutes in the preheated oven until the plums are tender. The exact cooking time depends on the size and ripeness of the fruit. Let cool for 15 minutes, then remove the rosemary.

3. Meanwhile, whip the cream until it holds soft peaks. Add the yogurt and gently fold together.

4. To serve, divide the warm plums and their syrupy juices among four bowls. Add a large spoonful of the yogurt mixture to each bowl and sprinkle with the muesli.

TO SERVE

To vary the flavor, replace the rosemary with a split vanilla bean or cinnamon sticks.

Oatmeal with Fruit & Nuts

 SERVES 2

 PREP TIME:
10 minutes

COOKING TIME:
8 minutes

nutritional information
per serving | 361 cal, 10.5g fat, 2g sat fat, 24g total sugars, 0.5g salt

Try this recipe to turn ordinary oatmeal into a bowl of sunshine to brighten your day.

INGREDIENTS

1 cup rolled oats

1¼ cups water

pinch of salt

⅓ cup mixed tropical dried fruit
and chopped nuts

1 large or 2 small bananas

reduced-fat coconut milk,
to serve

1. Put the oats into a nonstick saucepan and add the water and salt. Stir well and bring to a boil, then reduce the heat and simmer, stirring often, for 5 minutes, until the oatmeal is thick and fairly smooth.

2. When the oatmeal is nearly ready, stir in the mixed tropical fruit and nuts and cook for an additional minute.

3. Spoon the oatmeal into two serving bowls. Peel the banana and slice it over the the oatmeal. Serve immediately with reduced-fat coconut milk.

COOK'S NOTE

Cans of reduced-fat coconut milk, labeled "lite" or "light," are sold at grocery stores.

Fresh Croissants

 MAKES 12

 PREP TIME:
40 minutes
plus rising

COOKING TIME:
15–20 minutes

nutritional information per croissant	372 cal, 23g fat, 14g sat fat, 5g total sugars, 0.8g salt

You could start this recipe the night before. Make the dough and roll out the croissants, then brush with the glaze, cover with plastic wrap, and refrigerate overnight. The next morning, let rise for 30-45 minutes, then bake.

INGREDIENTS

3⅔ cups white bread flour, plus extra for rolling

3 tablespoons sugar

1 teaspoon salt

2 teaspoons active dry yeast

1¼ cups milk, heated until just warm to the touch

2½ sticks butter, softened, plus extra for greasing

1 egg, lightly beaten with 1 tablespoon milk, for glazing

strawberry preserves, to serve

1. Stir the dry ingredients into a large mixing bowl, make a well in the center, and add the milk. Mix to a soft dough, adding more milk if too dry. Knead on a lightly floured surface for 5–10 minutes, or until smooth and elastic. Let rise in a large greased bowl, covered, in a warm place until doubled in size. Meanwhile, flatten the butter with a rolling pin between two sheets of wax paper to form a rectangle about ¼ inch thick, then chill.

2. Knead the dough for 1 minute. Remove the butter from the refrigerator and let soften slightly. Roll out the dough on a well-floured surface to 18 x 6 inches. Place the butter in the center, folding up the sides and squeezing the edges together gently. With the short end of the dough toward you, fold the top third down toward the center, then fold the bottom third up. Rotate 90 degrees clockwise so that the fold is to your left and the top flap toward your right. Roll out to a rectangle and fold again. If the butter feels soft, wrap the dough in plastic wrap and chill. Repeat the rolling process two more times. Cut the dough in half. Roll out one half into a triangle ¼ inch thick (keep the other half refrigerated). Use a cardboard triangular template with a base of 7 inches and sides of 8 inches to cut out six croissants. Repeat with the other half of dough.

3. Preheat the oven to 400°F. Brush the triangles lightly with the glaze. Roll into croissant shapes, starting at the base and tucking the point underneath to prevent it from unrolling while cooking. Brush again with the glaze. Place on an ungreased baking sheet and let double in size. Bake for 15–20 minutes, until golden brown. Serve warm with strawberry preserves.

1

2

Strawberry Cream Cheese Spread

 SERVES 4   PREP TIME: 10 minutes   COOKING TIME: No cooking

nutritional information per serving	166 cal, 5g fat, 3g sat fat, 13g total sugars, 0.4g salt

You can make a stunning display of sliced fruits to serve with this delicious dip.

INGREDIENTS

⅔ cup hulled, coarsely chopped ripe strawberries, plus extra to garnish

1 tablespoon confectioners' sugar

1 cup plain Greek-style yogurt

1 teaspoon lemon juice

4 slices whole-wheat bread

2 large pieces of fruit, such as a mango, nectarine, or banana, cut into wedges

1. Process the strawberries with the confectioners' sugar in a blender for a few seconds, or mash with the sugar using a fork.

2. Combine the mixture with the yogurt and lemon juice in a bowl. Spoon into a serving dish and chill, if you have time.

3. Toast the bread and cut into strips. Arrange the fruit and toast as dippers on a plate around the strawberry dip. Garnish the dip with half a fresh strawberry. Serve immediately.

1   2   3

SOMETHING
DIFFERENT
Serve small
shortbread
cookies with
the dip for
a delicious
dessert.

Eggs Florentine

 SERVES 4    PREP TIME: 20 minutes   COOKING TIME: 35–40 minutes

nutritional information per serving	477 cal, 39g fat, 16g sat fat, 7g total sugars, 1.1g salt

This classic dish is always a favorite for a special breakfast or a lazy weekend brunch.

INGREDIENTS

1 pound fresh spinach leaves, thoroughly washed

4 tablespoons unsalted butter, plus extra for greasing

¾ cup sliced white button mushrooms

⅓ cup pine nuts, toasted

6 scallions, chopped

4 eggs

3 tablespoons whole-wheat flour

1¼ cups milk, warmed

1 teaspoon prepared English mustard

¾ cup shredded sharp vegetarian cheddar cheese

salt and pepper

1. Preheat the oven to 375°F. Shake off any excess water from the spinach, put into a large saucepan over medium heat with only the water clinging to the leaves, and sprinkle with a little salt. Cover and cook for 2–3 minutes, or until wilted. Drain, pressing out any excess liquid, then chop and place in a greased ovenproof dish.

2. Heat 1 tablespoon of the butter in a small saucepan over medium heat, add the mushrooms, and cook for 2 minutes, stirring frequently. Add the pine nuts and scallions and cook for an additional 2 minutes. Remove from the heat, season with salt and pepper, and spread the mixture over the spinach. Reserve and keep warm.

3. Meanwhile, fill a skillet with water and bring to a boil, then reduce the heat to a gentle simmer. Carefully break an egg into a cup and slip it into the water. Add the remaining eggs and cook for 4–5 minutes, or until set. Carefully remove with a slotted spoon and arrange on top of the spinach mixture.

4. Melt the remaining butter in a saucepan and stir in the flour. Cook for 2 minutes, then remove from the heat and gradually stir in the milk. Return to the heat and cook, stirring continuously, until the mixture comes to a boil and has thickened. Stir in the mustard, then ½ cup of the cheese. Continue stirring until the cheese has melted. Season with salt and pepper, then pour the sauce over the eggs, completely covering them. Sprinkle with the remaining cheese.

5. Cook in the preheated oven for 20–25 minutes, or until piping hot and the top is golden brown and bubbling. Serve immediately.

Muesli Pancake Stack with Honey

SERVES 4   **PREP TIME:** 15 minutes   **COOKING TIME:** 15 minutes

nutritional information per serving	385 cal, 14g fat, 3.5g sat fat, 9g total sugars, 0.9g salt

This is a recipe that combines two breakfast favorites in one neat package. Using different muesli recipes, the variations are endless.

INGREDIENTS

1¼ cups all-purpose white flour

1½ teaspoons baking powder

pinch of salt

1 cup milk

1 extra-large egg

2 tablespoons sunflower oil, plus extra for greasing

2 tablespoons plain low-fat yogurt

1⅔ cups muesli

honey, to serve

1. Sift the flour, baking powder, and salt into a bowl. Add the milk, egg, oil, and yogurt and beat to a smooth batter. Stir in the muesli and let stand for 5 minutes.

2. Lightly grease a flat griddle pan or skillet and heat over medium heat. Spoon tablespoons of batter onto the pan and cook until bubbles appear on the surface.

3. Turn over with a spatula and cook the other side until golden brown. Repeat this process using the remaining batter, while keeping the cooked pancakes warm.

4. Spoon honey over the pancakes and serve immediately.

SOMETHING
DIFFERENT
Try maple syrup
instead of honey
for a more
traditional flavor.

French Toast Waffles

 SERVES 4    PREP TIME: 15 minutes    COOKING TIME: 15 minutes

nutritional information per serving	536 cal, 19g fat, 11g sat fat, 20g total sugars, 1.4g salt

Similar to the traditional favorite French toast, but when cooked in a waffle maker you create an altogether more impressive dish. Alternatively, cook in a skillet or in the oven on a baking sheet.

INGREDIENTS

1¼ cups all-purpose white flour
1½ teaspoons baking powder
pinch of salt
1 teaspoon ground cinnamon
2 tablespoons sugar
1 cup milk
1 extra-large egg
2 tablespoons melted butter, plus extra to serve
sunflower oil, for greasing
8–10 slices brioche-type bread
raw or granulated sugar, to serve

1. Sift the flour, baking powder, salt, cinnamon, and sugar into a bowl. Add the milk, egg, and butter and beat to a smooth batter. Let stand for 5 minutes.

2. Lightly grease a waffle maker with the oil and heat until hot. Dip the slices of bread quickly into the batter, then place in the waffle maker and cook until golden brown. Repeat, using the remaining batter and bread, while keeping the cooked waffles warm.

3. Serve immediately, with melted butter and sugar.

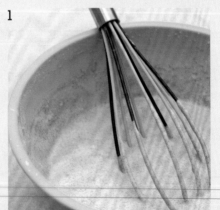

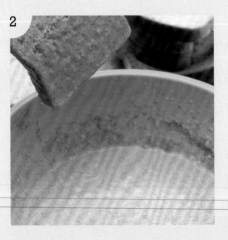

BE PREPARED

Make waffles in advance and reheat in a medium hot oven when required.

Pancake Eggs Benedict

 SERVES 4   PREP TIME: 15 minutes    COOKING TIME: 15 minutes

nutritional information per serving	350 cal, 17g fat, 5g sat fat, 3g total sugars, 1.1g salt

This combination of two traditional dishes deserves a generous helping of a classic hollandaise sauce.

INGREDIENTS

1¼ cups all-purpose white flour
1½ teaspoons baking powder
pinch of salt
1 cup milk
1 extra-large egg
2 tablespoons melted butter
sunflower oil, for greasing

topping
4 extra-large eggs

hollandaise sauce
3 egg yolks
½ teaspoon English mustard
1 tablespoon lemon juice
1¾ sticks butter
salt and pepper

1. Sift the flour, baking powder, and salt into a bowl. Add the milk, egg, and butter and beat to a smooth batter. Let stand for 5 minutes.

2. Lightly grease a flat griddle pan or skillet with the oil and heat over medium heat. Spoon tablespoons of batter onto the pan and cook until bubbles appear on the surface.

3. Turn over with a spatula and cook the other side until golden brown. Repeat this process using the remaining batter, while keeping the cooked pancakes warm.

4. For the topping, bring a wide saucepan of water to a boil, then reduce the heat to low simmer. Carefully break the eggs into the water and poach for about 3 minutes, until the whites are set but the yolks are still runny.

5. Meanwhile, make the sauce. Place the egg yolks, mustard and lemon juice in a blender and blend for a few seconds until smooth. Place the butter in a saucepan and heat until bubbling. With the motor running, gradually pour the butter into the egg yolks until the sauce is thickened and creamy. Season with salt and pepper.

6. Place three overlapping pancakes on each plate with an egg on top. Place the egg yolks, mustard and lemon juice in a blender and blend for a few seconds until smooth. Spoon over the sauce, season with salt and pepper, and serve immediately.

Pancakes with Baked Mushrooms

 SERVES 6   PREP TIME: 15 minutes   COOKING TIME: 15 minutes

nutritional information per serving	295 cal, 21g fat, 10g sat fat, 2.5g total sugars, 0.8g salt

The aroma from melted herb butter with garlic oil on mushrooms will get the taste buds tingling.

INGREDIENTS

1¼ cups all-purpose white flour
1½ teaspoons baking powder
pinch of salt
1 cup milk
1 extra-large egg
2 tablespoons melted butter
sunflower oil, for greasing

topping
4 tablespoons butter
2 tablespoons chopped fresh parsley
1 tablespoon snipped chives
1 garlic clove, crushed
3 tablespoons olive oil
12 portobello mushrooms
salt and pepper

1. For the topping, preheat the oven to 400°F. Beat the butter until softened, stir in the parsley and chives, and season with salt and pepper.

2. Mix together the garlic and oil. Place the mushrooms on a baking sheet in a single layer, brush with the garlic oil, and season with salt and pepper. Bake in the oven for about 15 minutes, turning once, until tender.

3. Meanwhile, sift the flour, baking powder, and salt into a bowl. Add the milk, egg, and butter and beat to a smooth batter. Let stand for 5 minutes.

4. Lightly grease a flat griddle pan or skillet and heat over medium heat. Spoon tablespoons of batter onto the pan and cook until bubbles appear on the surface.

5. Turn over with a spatula and cook the other side until golden brown. Repeat this process using the remaining batter, while keeping the cooked pancakes warm.

6. Place a mushroom on each pancake, top with a spoonful of herb butter, and serve immediately.

Croissants with Berries & Mascarpone

 SERVES 4

PREP TIME:
40 minutes
plus cooling

COOKING TIME:
3–4 minutes

nutritional information per serving	460 cal, 33g fat, 20g sat fat, 11.5g total sugars, 0.7g salt

These croissants are quick to assemble, and everyone will think you've gone to a lot more effort than you have!

INGREDIENTS

4 croissants

½ vanilla bean

¾ cup vegetarian mascarpone cheese

1 tablespoon confectioners' sugar, plus extra for dusting

¼ cup light cream

1½ cups prepared berries, such as strawberries, blueberries, and raspberries

1. Preheat the oven to 400°F. Slice through the croissants horizontally, then reassemble them and place on a baking sheet. Warm them in the preheated oven for 3–4 minutes.

2. Scrape the seeds from the vanilla bean into a small bowl. Add the mascarpone cheese, confectioners' sugar, and 2 tablespoons of the cream. Beat together until smooth, then beat in the remaining cream.

3. Open up the warmed croissants. Divide the mascarpone mixture and the fruit among the croissant bottoms, then replace the lids. Sift a little confectioners' sugar over the top and serve immediately.

1   2   3

SOMETHING
DIFFERENT
In fall and
winter, replace
the berries with
stewed apple or
toasted slivered
almonds.

Zucchini Fritters with Eggs & Caramelized Onions

SERVES 4

PREP TIME:
40 minutes
plus cooling

COOKING TIME:
45 minutes

nutritional information per serving	572 cal, 33g fat, 6g sat fat, 14g total sugars, 0.8g salt

Make the caramelized onions in advance and store in the refrigerator for up to a week. If the batter for the fritters seems too thick, stir in a little extra milk.

INGREDIENTS

2 tablespoons extra virgin olive oil

5 red onions, sliced

1 tablespoon brown sugar

1⅔ cups all-purpose white flour

2½ teaspoons baking powder

1 egg, lightly beaten, plus 4 eggs for poaching or frying

1 cup milk

2 zucchini, shredded

1 cup sunflower oil

salt and pepper

1. Heat the olive oil in a large, heavy saucepan over medium heat, add the onions, and cook for 5 minutes, or until softened. Stir in the sugar and reduce the heat, cover, and cook for 30 minutes, or until the onions are deep brown in color, stirring occasionally. Season with salt and pepper and let cool.

2. To make the fritters, sift the flour and baking powder into a large bowl and make a well in the center. Mix together the beaten egg and milk and incorporate into the flour, using a wooden spoon to make a batter. Season with salt and pepper and stir in the shredded zucchini.

3. Heat the sunflower oil in a wide, deep saucepan and drop in tablespoons of the batter. Cook until golden brown on both sides, turning once. Drain on paper towels and keep warm.

4. Poach or fry the eggs, as you prefer. To serve, place three fritters on each individual plate, place an egg on top, and spoon some of the caramelized onions over the eggs. Serve immediately.

Asparagus & Egg Pastries

 SERVES 4

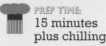 PREP TIME:
15 minutes
plus chilling

 COOKING TIME:
20–25 minutes

nutritional information per serving	600 cal, 37g fat, 16g sat fat, 6g total sugars, 1.7g salt

Spicy smoked paprika is the perfect complement to these baked eggs in puff pastry.

INGREDIENTS

1 sheet ready-to-bake puff pastry

flour, for dusting

milk, for brushing

10 ounces slim asparagus spears

¾ cup prepared tomato-based pasta sauce

1 teaspoon hot smoked paprika

4 eggs

salt and pepper

1. Roll out the pastry on a lightly floured surface to a 15 x 10-inch rectangle, then cut into four pieces to make 7½ x 5-inch rectangles. Line a baking sheet with nonstick parchment paper and place the pastry rectangles on the sheet. Prick all over with a fork and brush lightly with milk. Chill for 20 minutes.

2. Meanwhile, preheat the oven to 400°F. Snap the woody ends off the asparagus and discard. Bring a saucepan of lightly salted water to a boil, then add the asparagus, bring back to a boil, and cook for 2–3 minutes, until almost tender. Drain and refresh in cold water, then drain again.

3. Mix the tomato sauce and paprika together and divide among the pastries, spreading it out almost to the edges. Bake in the preheated oven for 10–12 minutes, until the pastry is puffed around the edges and pale golden.

4. Remove from the oven and arrange the asparagus on top of the pastries, leaving space for the egg in the middle of each pastry. Crack one egg into a cup and slide into the space created in one of the pastries. Repeat with the remaining eggs, then return the pastries to the oven for 8 minutes, or until the eggs are just set. Season with salt and pepper and serve immediately.

GOES WELL WITH

Serve warm naan bread or crispy poppadoms as an accompaniment.

Spicy Zucchini Soup
with Rice & Lime

SERVES 4

PREP TIME:
10 minutes

COOKING TIME:
20 minutes

nutritional information per serving	195 cal, 6g fat, 0.7g sat fat, 0.8g total sugars, 1g salt

A squeeze of lime added to this light, fresh tasting soup makes all the difference.

INGREDIENTS

2 tablespoons vegetable oil

4 garlic cloves, thinly sliced

1–2 tablespoons mild chili powder

¼ –½ teaspoon ground cumin

6½ cups vegetable stock

2 zucchini, cut into bite-size chunks

¼ cup long-grain rice

salt and pepper

fresh oregano sprigs, to garnish

lime wedges, to serve

1. Heat the oil in a heavy saucepan. Add the garlic and cook for 2 minutes, or until softened. Add the chili powder and cumin and cook over medium–low heat for 1 minute.

2. Stir in the stock, zucchini, and rice, then cook over medium–high heat for 10 minutes, or until the zucchini is just tender and the rice is cooked through. Season with salt and pepper.

3. Ladle into warm bowls, garnish with oregano sprigs, and serve immediately with lime wedges.

SOMETHING
DIFFERENT
Use a combination
of green and
yellow zucchini
for extra color.

Pea & Herb Soup
with Basil Oil

 SERVES 4 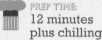 PREP TIME: 12 minutes plus chilling COOKING TIME: 15–20 minutes

nutritional information **per serving** — 277 cal, 22g fat, 8g sat fat, 4g total sugars, 0.2g salt

This elegant soup is delicious hot or chilled.

INGREDIENTS

2 tablespoons butter

6 scallions, chopped

1 celery stalk, finely chopped

2½ cups frozen peas or fresh shelled peas

3 cups vegetable stock

2 tablespoons chopped fresh dill

1 tablespoon snipped fresh chives

2 cups arugula

2 tablespoons crème fraîche or Greek-style yogurt

salt and pepper

bread sticks, to serve

basil oil

½ bunch of basil

1 cup olive oil

1. Melt the butter in a saucepan over medium heat. Add the scallions and celery, cover, and cook for 5 minutes, until soft. Add the peas and stock, bring to a boil, and simmer for 10 minutes. Remove from the heat. Cover and let cool for 20 minutes.

2. To make the basil oil, remove the stems from the basil and discard. Place the leaves in a food processor with half the oil and blend to a puree. Add the remaining oil and blend again. Transfer to a small bowl.

3. Add the dill, chives, and arugula to the soup. Blend with a handheld immersion blender until smooth. Stir in the crème fraîche. If serving warm, heat through gently without boiling, then season to taste.

4. Ladle into four warm bowls and drizzle with the basil oil. Serve immediately, with bread sticks on the side. If serving chilled, let cool completely, then chill in the refrigerator for at least 1 hour before checking the seasoning and serving.

1

2

3

COOK'S NOTE
Any leftover basil oil can be stored in the refrigerator for 3-4 days and used for drizzling over salads or ciabatta or tossing with pasta.

Vegetable & Corn Chowder

 SERVES 4   PREP TIME: 10 minutes   COOKING TIME: 25–30 minutes

nutritional information per serving — 363 cal, 16g fat, 8g sat fat, 14g total sugars, 0.8g salt

Chowder is traditionally from New England and is another name for a thick, hearty soup.

INGREDIENTS

1 tablespoon vegetable oil

1 red onion, diced

1 red bell pepper, seeded and diced

3 garlic cloves, crushed

2 cups peeled, diced Yukon gold or white round potatoes

2 tablespoons all-purpose flour

2½ cups whole milk

1¼ cups vegetable stock

¾ cup broccoli florets

1 (11-ounce) can corn kernels, drained

⅔ cup shredded vegetarian cheddar cheese

salt and pepper

1. Heat the oil in a large saucepan. Add the onion, red bell pepper, garlic, and potatoes and sauté over low heat, stirring frequently, for 2–3 minutes.

2. Stir in the flour and cook, stirring, for 30 seconds. Gradually stir in the milk and stock.

3. Add the broccoli and corn kernels. Bring the mixture to a boil, stirring continuously, then reduce the heat and simmer for about 20 minutes, or until all the vegetables are tender.

4. Stir in ½ cup of the cheese until it melts. Season to taste and ladle into warm bowls. Garnish with the remaining cheese and serve immediately.

GOES WELL WITH
Serve with crusty sourdough or whole-grain bread for a satisfying lunch.

Roasted Squash Soup with Cheese-Topped Toasts

SERVES 4

PREP TIME:
20 minutes

COOKING TIME:
1 hour

nutritional information per serving	548 cal, 26g fat, 13g sat fat, 16g total sugars, 1.4g salt

A comforting, velvety textured soup that's perfect for freezing.

INGREDIENTS

1 butternut squash, cut into small chunks

2 onions, cut into wedges

2 tablespoons olive oil

2 garlic cloves, crushed

3–4 fresh thyme sprigs, leaves removed

4 cups vegetable stock

⅔ cup crème fraîche or Greek-style yogurt

salt and pepper

snipped fresh chives, to garnish

toasts

1 baguette, thinly sliced diagonally

½ cup grated vegetarian hard cheese

1. Preheat the oven to 375°F. Place the squash, onions, oil, garlic, and thyme leaves in a roasting pan. Toss together and spread out in a single layer. Roast for 50–60 minutes, stirring occasionally, until the vegetables are tender and caramelized in places.

2. Transfer the vegetables to a saucepan. Add half the stock and puree with a handheld immersion blender until smooth. Alternatively, blend in a food processor, then transfer to a saucepan. Stir in the remaining stock and crème fraîche. Season with salt and pepper, and heat through gently.

3. To make the toasts, preheat the broiler to high. Toast the sliced baguette under the preheated broiler for 1–2 minutes on each side, until pale golden. Sprinkle with the cheese and return to the broiler for an additional 30–40 seconds, until melted and bubbling.

4. Ladle the soup into four warm bowls and sprinkle with chives to garnish. Serve immediately with the cheese toasts on the side.

Thai Noodle Soup

 SERVES 4   PREP TIME: 25 minutes   COOKING TIME: 10–15 minutes

nutritional information
per serving   177 cal, 5.5g fat, 0.4g sat fat, 2g total sugars, 0.9g salt

Try this light, spicy soup at the beginning of a Thai-inspired meal—it will awaken the taste buds. Shiitake mushrooms provide an authentic flavor and are available in larger supermarkets or Asian stores.

INGREDIENTS

½ ounce dried shiitake mushrooms

5 cups vegetable stock

1 tablespoon peanut oil

4 scallions, sliced

8 baby corn, sliced

2 garlic cloves, crushed

2 fresh kaffir lime leaves, chopped

2 tablespoons red curry paste

3 ounces rice vermicelli noodles

1 tablespoon light soy sauce

2 tablespoons chopped cilantro, to garnish

1. Place the mushrooms in a bowl, cover with the vegetable stock, and let soak for 20 minutes.

2. Heat the peanut oil in a saucepan over medium heat. Add the scallions, baby corn, garlic, and kaffir lime leaves. Sauté for 3 minutes to soften.

3. Add the red curry paste and the soaked mushrooms and their soaking liquid. Bring to a boil and simmer for 5 minutes, stirring occasionally.

4. Add the noodles and soy sauce to the red curry mixture in the pan. Return the pan to a boil and simmer for an additional 4 minutes, until the noodles are just cooked. Ladle into warm bowls, garnish with the chopped cilantro, and serve immediately.

1

2

3

SOMETHING DIFFERENT
Use one or two ears
of corn instead of
baby corn. Stand
the cobs upright on
a board and, with a
sharp knife, cut down
from the top to remove
all the kernels.

Spicy Pea Soup

 SERVES 4   PREP TIME: 5 minutes   COOKING TIME: 35–40 minutes

nutritional information per serving	235 cal, 6g fat, 0.8g sat fat, 2g total sugars, trace salt

Just the recipe when you want a simple soup packed with great flavors.

INGREDIENTS

4 cups water

1¼ cups pigeon peas or black-eyed peas

1 teaspoon paprika

½ teaspoon chili powder

½ teaspoon ground turmeric

2 tablespoons ghee or vegetable oil

1 fresh green chile, seeded and finely chopped

1 teaspoon cumin seeds

3 curry leaves, roughly torn

1 teaspoon sugar

salt

1 teaspoon garam masala, to garnish

1. Bring the water to a boil in a large, heavy saucepan. Add the dried peas, cover, and simmer, stirring occasionally, for 25 minutes.

2. Stir in the paprika, chili powder, and turmeric, replace the lid, and cook for an additional 10 minutes, or until the peas are tender.

3. Meanwhile, heat the ghee in a small skillet. Add the chile, cumin seeds, and curry leaves and cook, stirring continuously, for 1 minute.

4. Add the spice mixture to the peas. Stir in the sugar and season with salt. Ladle into warm bowls, garnish with garam masala, and serve immediately.

FREEZING TIP
If you find a fresh supply of curry leaves, it's worth freezing them in a zip-topped bag to save for another dish that calls for the ingredient.

Pea & Bean Soup

 SERVES 4

 PREP TIME:
10 minutes

COOKING TIME:
25–30 minutes

nutritional information per serving	176 cal, 6g fat, 0.8g sat fat, 3.5g total sugars, 0.7g salt

A delicious summery soup, especially if you are lucky enough to have peas growing in your yard.

INGREDIENTS

1½ tablespoons olive oil

1 bunch scallions, chopped

1 large celery stalk, chopped

1 garlic clove, crushed

1 Yukon gold or white round potato, peeled and diced

5 cups vegetable stock

1 bay leaf

1 cup peas

1 (15-ounce) can cranberry beans, drained and rinsed

salt and pepper

finely shredded fresh mint, to garnish

multigrain bread rolls, to serve

1. Heat the oil in a large saucepan over medium–high heat. Add the scallions, celery, and garlic and cook, stirring, for about 3 minutes, or until soft. Add the potato and stir for an additional minute.

2. Add the stock and bay leaf. Season with salt and pepper and bring to a boil, stirring. Reduce the heat to low, cover the pan, and simmer for 20 minutes, or until the potatoes are tender.

3. Add the peas and beans and return the soup to a boil. Reduce the heat, replace the lid on the pan, and continue to simmer until the peas are tender.

4. Remove and discard the bay leaf, then transfer the soup to a food processor or blender and process until smooth. Place a metal strainer over the rinsed-out pan and use a wooden spoon to push the soup through the strainer.

5. Reheat gently. Ladle the soup into warm bowls, garnish with mint, and serve immediately with bread rolls.

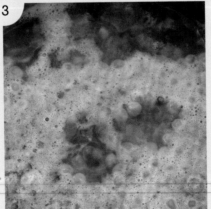

White Bean Soup

 SERVES 4

 PREP TIME:
10 minutes
plus soaking

COOKING TIME:
2 hours 20 minutes

nutritional information per serving	384 cal, 18g fat, 2.5g sat fat, 1.5g total sugars, trace salt

A traditional Italian rustic soup from Tuscany, prepare the day before because the flavors will improve.

INGREDIENTS

1 cup dried cannellini beans, soaked in cold water to cover overnight

6½ cups vegetable stock

4 ounces dried corallini, conchigliette piccole, or other soup pasta

⅓ cup olive oil

2 garlic cloves, finely chopped

¼ cup chopped fresh flat-leaf parsley

salt and pepper

fresh crusty bread, to serve

1. Drain the soaked beans, rinse, and place them in a large, heavy saucepan. Add the stock and bring to a boil. Partly cover the pan, then reduce the heat and simmer for 2 hours, or until tender.

2. Transfer about half the beans and a little of the stock to a food processor or blender and process to a smooth puree. Return the puree to the pan and stir well to mix. Return to a boil.

3. Add the pasta, return to a boil, and cook for 10 minutes, or according to the package directions, until tender.

4. Meanwhile, heat ¼ cup of the olive oil in a small saucepan. Add the garlic and cook over low heat, stirring frequently, for 4–5 minutes, or until golden. Stir the garlic mixture into the soup and add the parsley. Season with salt and pepper and ladle into warm bowls. Drizzle with the remaining olive oil and serve immediately with crusty bread.

GOES WELL WITH
Salad greens
tossed with
balsamic dressing
and topped
with shavings
of cheese.

Vichyssoise

 SERVES 6

 PREP TIME:
40 minutes
plus chilling

 COOKING TIME:
35 minutes

nutritional information
per serving   309 cal, 22g fat, 14g sat fat, 8g total sugars, 0.3g salt

*A really delicious chilled soup for summer entertaining,
but equally good served hot when the weather is chilly.*

INGREDIENTS

1 pound leeks, white parts only

4 potatoes

4 tablespoons butter

5 cups water

2½ cups whole milk

1¼ cups sour cream,
plus extra to garnish

salt and pepper

2 tablespoons snipped fresh
chives, to garnish

1. Thinly slice the leeks. Peel and dice the potatoes. Melt the butter in a large, heavy saucepan over low heat. Add the leeks, cover, and cook, stirring occasionally, for 10 minutes.

2. Stir in the potatoes and cook over medium heat, stirring frequently, for 2 minutes. Pour in the water and add a pinch of salt. Bring to a boil, then reduce the heat and simmer for 15–20 minutes, until the potatoes are tender. Remove from the heat and let cool slightly. Transfer to a blender or food processor and process into a puree. Push the mixture through a strainer into a clean saucepan with a wooden spoon, then stir in the milk. Season with salt and pepper and stir in half the sour cream.

3. Reheat the soup, then push through a strainer into a bowl. Stir in the remaining cream, cover with plastic wrap, and let cool. Chill in the refrigerator for 4–8 hours. Serve in chilled bowls, with swirls of sour cream and chives to garnish.

FREEZING TIP
Freeze for up
to three months.
Defrost complete-
ly and stir well
before serving
cold or reheat
gently.

French Onion Soup

 SERVES 6   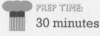 PREP TIME: 30 minutes   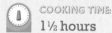 COOKING TIME: 1½ hours

nutritional information
per serving | 432 cal, 24g fat, 11g sat fat, 8g total sugars, 1.4g salt

Traditionally, this soup is served throughout the night to workers at the famous Les Halles market in Paris.

INGREDIENTS

6 onions

3 tablespoons olive oil

4 garlic cloves, 3 chopped and 1 peeled but kept whole

1 teaspoon sugar

2 teaspoons chopped fresh thyme, plus extra sprigs to garnish

2 tablespoons all-purpose flour

½ cup dry white wine

9 cups vegetable stock

6 slices French bread

2 cups shredded vegetarian Gruyère cheese,

1. Thinly slice the onions. Heat the oil in a large, heavy saucepan over medium–low heat, add the onions, and cook, stirring occasionally, for 10 minutes, or until they are just beginning to brown. Stir in the chopped garlic, sugar, and chopped thyme, then reduce the heat and cook, stirring occasionally, for 30 minutes, or until the onions are golden brown.

2. Sprinkle in the flour and cook, stirring continuously, for 1–2 minutes. Stir in the wine. Gradually stir in the stock and bring to a boil, skimming off any foam that rises to the surface, then reduce the heat and simmer for 45 minutes. Meanwhile, preheat the broiler to medium–high. Toast the bread on both sides under the broiler, then rub the toast with the whole garlic clove.

3. Ladle the soup into six flameproof bowls set on a baking sheet. Float a piece of toast in each bowl and divide the shredded cheese among them. Place under the broiler for 2–3 minutes, or until the cheese has just melted. Garnish with thyme sprigs and serve immediately.

1

2

3

COOK'S NOTE

Plan for plenty of time to make the soup ahead because the flavor will develop if it is left to stand.

Mini Roasted Vegetable Kabobs

 SERVES 4    PREP TIME: 10 minutes   COOKING TIME: 25–30 minutes

nutritional information per serving   135 cal, 8g fat, 2g sat fat, 10g total sugars, 0.2g salt

Roasting vegetables in the oven brings out their natural sweetness and the pieces stay in neat shapes, too.

INGREDIENTS

1 red bell pepper, seeded
1 yellow bell pepper, seeded
1 large zucchini
1 eggplant
2 tablespoons olive oil
3 garlic cloves, crushed
salt and pepper

dip

2 tablespoons chopped fresh dill
2 tablespoons chopped fresh mint
1 cup plain yogurt

1. Preheat the oven to 400°F. Cut the vegetables into ¾-inch chunks. Place in a roasting pan large enough to hold them in a single layer.

2. Mix together the olive oil and garlic and drizzle the mixture over the vegetables. Season well with salt and pepper, then toss together. Roast for 25–30 minutes, until tender and lightly charred.

3. Meanwhile, stir the dill and mint into the yogurt. Spoon into four serving bowls.

4. When the vegetables are cool enough to handle, divide them among 12 long toothpicks or short skewers. Serve warm or cold with the bowls of dip on the side.

BE PREPARED
Cut the vegetables into
chunks in advance and
marinate for several
hours or overnight.

Eggplant Pâté

 SERVES 6

 PREP TIME:
10 minutes
plus cooling

 COOKING TIME:
1¼ hours

nutritional information per serving: 73 cal, 7.5g fat, 1g sat fat, 1g total sugars, trace salt

Also known as Poor Man's Caviar because the humble eggplant, when prepared this way, tastes so delicious!

INGREDIENTS

2 large eggplants

¼ cup extra virgin olive oil

2 garlic cloves, finely chopped

¼ cup lemon juice

salt and pepper

2 tablespoons coarsely chopped fresh flat-leaf parsley, to garnish

6 crisp breads, to serve

1. Preheat the oven to 350°F. Score the skins of the eggplants with the point of a sharp knife, without piercing the flesh, and place them on a baking sheet. Bake for 1¼ hours, or until soft.

2. Remove the eggplants from the oven and let stand until cool enough to handle. Cut them in half and, using a spoon, scoop out the flesh into a bowl. Mash the flesh thoroughly.

3. Gradually beat in the olive oil, then stir in the garlic and lemon juice. Season with salt and pepper. Cover with plastic wrap and store in the refrigerator until required. Sprinkle with the parsley and serve with crisp breads.

1

2

3

COOK'S NOTE
Makes a great
dip, too, served
with sticks of
carrot, celery,
and bell pepper.

Blue Cheese & Herb Pâté

 SERVES 4  PREP TIME: 15 minutes plus chilling 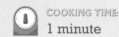 COOKING TIME: 1 minute

nutritional information per serving	509 cal, 42g fat, 25g sat fat, 5g total sugars, 1.3g salt

If you need something to serve as an appetizer or pack for a picnic, this pâté is ideal.

INGREDIENTS

⅔ cup vegetarian low-fat cream cheese

1½ cups Greek-style yogurt

1 cup crumbled vegetarian blue cheese

⅓ cup dried cranberries, finely chopped

⅓ cup chopped fresh herbs, such as parsley, chives, dill, and tarragon

6 tablespoons butter

2 tablespoons chopped walnuts

whole-grain toast or bread sticks, to serve

1. Beat the cream cheese to soften, then gradually beat in the yogurt until smooth. Add the blue cheese, cranberries, and herbs. Stir together. Spoon the mixture into four ⅔-cup ramekins (individual ceramic dishes) or small dishes and carefully smooth the tops.

2. Clarify the butter by gently heating it in a small saucepan until melted. Skim any foam off the surface and discard. Carefully pour the clear yellow top layer into a small bowl, leaving the milky liquid in the pan. The yellow layer is the clarified butter. Discard the liquid left in the pan.

3. Pour a little of the clarified butter over the top of each pâté and sprinkle with the walnuts. Chill for at least 30 minutes, until firm. Serve with whole-grain toast.

SOMETHING
DIFFERENT
The blue cheese
can be replaced
with tangy
vegetarian goat
cheese, if you
prefer.

Couscous with Roasted Cherry Tomatoes & Pine Nuts

 SERVES 4

 PREP TIME: 10 minutes plus standing

COOKING TIME: 8 minutes

nutritional information per serving	210 cal, 14g fat, 1.5g sat fat, 2.5g total sugars, trace salt

This looks really pretty made with mixed red and yellow cherry tomatoes.

INGREDIENTS

2 cups cherry tomatoes
3 tablespoons olive oil
⅔ cup couscous
1 cup boiling water
¼ cup pine nuts, toasted
⅓ cup coarsely chopped fresh mint
finely grated zest of 1 lemon
½ tablespoon lemon juice
salt and pepper

1. Preheat the oven to 425°F. Place the tomatoes and 1 tablespoon of the oil in an ovenproof dish. Toss together, then roast for 7–8 minutes in the preheated oven, until the tomatoes are soft and the skins have burst. Let stand for 5 minutes.

2. Put the couscous in a heatproof bowl. Pour over the boiling water, cover, and let stand for 8–10 minutes, until soft and the liquid is absorbed. Fluff up with a fork.

3. Add the tomatoes and their juices, the pine nuts, mint, lemon zest, lemon juice, and the remaining oil to the couscous. Season with salt and pepper, then gently toss together. Serve warm or cold.

1   1   2

GOES WELL WITH
This goes well
with a crisp
green salad and
some vegetarian
feta cheese or
charbroiled
halloumi.

Batter Fried Vegetables

 SERVES 4   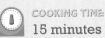 PREP TIME: 20 minutes   COOKING TIME: 15 minutes

nutritional information per serving	236 cal, 12g fat, 1.5g sat fat, 4g total sugars, 0.6g salt

Serve these crunchy vegetable fritters piping hot as a snack or part of an Indian-inspired meal.

INGREDIENTS

⅓ cup chickpea (besan) flour
½ teaspoon salt
1 teaspoon chili powder
1 teaspoon baking powder
1½ teaspoons white cumin seeds
1 teaspoon pomegranate seeds
1¼ cups water
¼ bunch of cilantro, finely chopped, plus extra sprigs to garnish

vegetables of your choice
cauliflower, cut into small florets; onions, cut into rings; potatoes, sliced; eggplants, sliced; or fresh spinach leaves

vegetable oil, for deep-frying

1. Sift the chickpea flour into a large bowl. Add the salt, chili powder, baking powder, cumin, and pomegranate seeds and blend together well. Pour in the water and beat well to form a smooth batter. Add the chopped cilantro and mix well, then set aside.

2. Dip the prepared vegetables into the batter, carefully shaking off any excess.

3. Heat enough oil for deep-frying in a wok, deep-fat fryer, or a large, heavy saucepan until it reaches 350°F, or until a cube of bread browns in 30 seconds. Using tongs, place the battered vegetables in the oil and deep-fry, in batches, turning once.

4. Repeat this process until all of the batter has been used. Transfer the battered vegetables to crumpled paper towels and drain thoroughly. Garnish with cilantro sprigs and serve immediately.

COOK'S NOTE

As the pakoras cook, transfer them to a wire rack placed on a baking sheet in medium-hot oven to keep warm until all the batches are cooked.

Roasted Vegetable & Feta Cheese Wraps

 SERVES 4

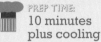 PREP TIME:
10 minutes
plus cooling

COOKING TIME:
15–20 minutes

nutritional information per serving	373 cal, 20g fat, 7g sat fat, 5g total sugars, 2.4g salt

Wraps are very convenient, and this is one of the many delicious combinations you can fill them with.

INGREDIENTS

1 red onion, cut into eighths

1 red bell pepper, seeded and cut into eighths

1 small eggplant, cut into eighths

1 zucchini, cut into eighths

¼ cup extra virgin olive oil

1 garlic clove, crushed

⅔ cup crumbled, drained vegetarian feta cheese

small bunch of fresh mint, shredded

4 sun-dried tomato wraps, 10 inches in diameter

salt and pepper

1. Preheat the oven to 425°F. Mix together all of the vegetables, olive oil, garlic, and salt and pepper and place in the oven in a nonstick baking sheet. Roast for 15–20 minutes, or until golden and cooked all the way through.

2. Remove from the oven, let cool, then mix in the feta and mint.

3. Preheat a nonstick pan or broiler pan until almost smoking, then cook the wraps one at a time on both sides for 10 seconds. This will add some color and also soften the wraps.

4. Divide the vegetable-and-feta mixture among the wraps, placing it along the middle of each wrap. Roll up the wrap, cut them in half, and serve immediately.

SOMETHING
DIFFERENT
You could spread
a spicy salsa
or creamy
hummus on the
wrap before
filling with the
other ingredients.

Hot & Sour Zucchini

 SERVES 4

PREP TIME:
30 minutes

COOKING TIME:
5 minutes

nutritional information per serving	86 cal, 7g fat, 1.5g sat fat, 4g total sugars, 1.9g salt

In a traditional Sichuan style, this is just one more way to serve the humble zucchini.

INGREDIENTS

2 large zucchini, thinly sliced

1 teaspoon salt

2 tablespoons peanut oil

1 teaspoon Sichuan peppercorns, crushed

½ –1 red chile, seeded and sliced into thin strips

1 large garlic clove, thinly sliced

½ teaspoon minced fresh ginger

1 tablespoon rice vinegar

1 tablespoon light soy sauce

2 teaspoons sugar

1 scallion, green part included, thinly sliced

a few drops of sesame oil and 1 teaspoon sesame seeds, to garnish

1. Put the zucchini slices in a large colander and toss with the salt. Cover with a plate and put a weight on top. Let drain for 20 minutes. Rinse off the salt and spread out the slices on paper towels to dry.

2. Preheat a wok over high heat and add the peanut oil. Add the Sichuan peppercorns, chile, garlic, and ginger. Sauté for about 20 seconds, until the garlic is just beginning to color.

3. Add the zucchini slices and toss in the oil. Add the rice vinegar, soy sauce, and sugar, and stir-fry for 2 minutes. Add the scallion and stir-fry for 30 seconds. Garnish with the sesame oil and seeds, and serve immediately.

COOK'S NOTE

Don't forget to salt the zucchini because it helps to draw out the excess water that can make the dish soggy.

Spicy Avocado Dip

 SERVES 4   PREP TIME: 10 minutes   COOKING TIME: No cooking

nutritional information per serving	192 cal, 19g fat, 4g sat fat, 1g total sugars, trace salt

When choosing avocados for this great tasting dip, go for the crinkly skinned ones, which have a better flavor. Check the ripeness, they should just give slightly when pressed gently with your thumb.

INGREDIENTS

2 large avocados
juice of 1–2 limes
2 large garlic cloves, crushed
1 teaspoon mild chili powder, or to taste, plus extra to garnish
salt and pepper

1. Cut the avocados in half. Remove the pits and skin and discard.

2. Place the avocado flesh in a food processor with the juice of 1 or 2 limes, according to taste. Add the garlic and chili powder and process until smooth.

3. Season with salt and pepper. Transfer to a serving bowl, garnish with chili powder, and serve.

SOMETHING DIFFERENT

Add some diced, seeded tomatoes or cucumber to the mixture for added crunch.

Mushrooms with Garlic & Scallions

 SERVES 4

PREP TIME:
10 minutes
plus cooling

COOKING TIME:
1½ hours

nutritional information per serving	80 cal, 6g fat, 1g sat fat, 2g total sugars, trace salt

There may seem to be a huge amount of garlic in this recipe, but don't worry—when you roast whole bulbs in the oven in this way, they become milder, sweeter, and deliciously caramelized.

INGREDIENTS

2 garlic bulbs

2 tablespoons olive oil

12 ounces assorted mushrooms, such as cremini, open-cap, and chanterelles, halved if large

1 tablespoon chopped fresh parsley

8 scallions, cut into 1-inch lengths

salt and pepper

1. Preheat the oven to 350°F. Slice off the tops of the garlic bulbs and press down to loosen the cloves. Place them in an ovenproof dish and season with salt and pepper. Drizzle 2 teaspoons of the oil over the bulbs and roast for 30 minutes. Remove from the oven and drizzle with 1 teaspoon of the remaining oil. Return to the oven and roast for an additional 45 minutes. Remove the garlic from the oven and, when cool enough to handle, peel the cloves.

2. Tip the oil from the dish into a heavy skillet. Add the remaining oil and heat. Add the mushrooms and cook over medium heat, stirring frequently, for 4 minutes.

3. Add the garlic cloves, parsley, and scallions and cook, stirring frequently, for 5 minutes. Season with salt and pepper and serve immediately.

GOES WELL WITH
Serve on toasted
ciabatta bread or
with scrambled
eggs.

Feta, Lemon & Herb Dip

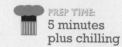 SERVES 5　 PREP TIME: 5 minutes plus chilling　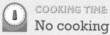 COOKING TIME: No cooking

nutritional information per serving	117 cal, 10g fat, 5g sat fat, 0.3g total sugars, 1g salt

This quickly made dip is also great served as an accompaniment to vegetable kabobs and baked potatoes.

INGREDIENTS

⅔ cup vegetarian low-fat cream cheese

3 tablespoons water

1 tablespoon olive oil

⅔ cup crumbled, drained vegetarian feta cheese

1 large lemon

3 tablespoons coarsely chopped fresh mint

3 tablespoons coarsely chopped fresh dill

pepper

a selection of vegetable sticks, to serve

1. Place the cream cheese, water, and oil in a food processor and process until smooth. Add the feta cheese and process briefly to combine, but make sure there are still some small lumps remaining. Transfer to a bowl.

2. Pare the zest from the lemon, using a zester. Stir the zest into the dip with the mint and dill. Season with pepper. Cover and chill for at least 30 minutes to let the flavors develop. Serve with a selection of vegetable sticks for dipping.

1

1

2

GET AHEAD
The dip and vegetable sticks can be prepared a day ahead and kept in the refrigerator.

Roasted Fennel with Cherry Tomatoes & Rosemary

 SERVES 4

PREP TIME:
5 minutes

COOKING TIME:
25–30 minutes

nutritional information per serving	100 cal, 7.5g fat, 1g sat fat, 3g total sugars, 0.2g salt

A wonderful side dish for the summer months when these vegetables are at their cheapest and best.

INGREDIENTS

4 fennel bulbs, cut into slim wedges

2 tablespoons olive oil

⅓ cup dry white wine

2 garlic cloves, crushed

2 teaspoons chopped fresh rosemary

12 cherry tomatoes

16 pitted ripe black olives

2 tablespoons chopped fresh parsley

salt and pepper

1. Preheat the oven to 400°F. Place the fennel in a roasting pan large enough to hold it in a single layer. Mix together the oil, 2 tablespoons of the wine, the garlic, and rosemary. Pour the mixture over the fennel, season with salt and pepper, and toss together.

2. Roast in the preheated oven for 15–20 minutes, until almost tender and lightly browned. Scatter the tomatoes and olives over the fennel. Pour over the remaining wine, then return to the oven for 8–10 minutes, until the tomatoes are soft and the skins have burst. Toss with the parsley and serve warm or cold.

GOES WELL WITH

To turn this side
dish into a light
meal, toss with
couscous and
toasted pine
nuts or with
pasta and
grated vegetarian
Parmesan-style
cheese.

Braised Peas with Lettuce & Tarragon

SERVES 4

PREP TIME:
5 minutes

COOKING TIME:
10–15 minutes

nutritional information per serving	162 cal, 8g fat, 3g sat fat, 3g total sugars, trace salt

Transform humble peas into a side dish fit for a dinner party with this quick recipe.

INGREDIENTS

1 tablespoon butter

1 tablespoon olive oil

1 leek, thinly sliced

2 teaspoons all-purpose flour

1 cup vegetable stock

2¼ cups fresh or frozen peas

2 Boston lettuce, sliced

3 tablespoons chopped fresh tarragon

1 tablespoon lemon juice

salt and pepper

1. Heat the butter and oil in a large saucepan. Add the leek, cover, and cook over low heat for 5 minutes, until soft. Stir in the flour, then gradually stir in the stock.

2. Add the peas, increase the heat, cover, and simmer for 4 minutes. Add the lettuce without stirring it in, cover, and simmer for an additional 2 minutes, until the vegetables are tender.

3. Stir the lettuce, tarragon, and lemon juice into the peas. Season with salt and pepper and serve immediately.

SOMETHING
DIFFERENT
To vary the flavor, replace the tarragon with mint or the lettuce with frisée endive.

Spinach & Herb Chutney with Olives

 SERVES 4

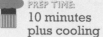 PREP TIME:
10 minutes
plus cooling

COOKING TIME:
15–20 minutes

nutritional information per serving	95 cal, 9.5g fat, 1.5g sat fat, 1g total sugars, 0.3g salt

With a vibrant green color and zingy combination of herbs and spices, this is perfect spread on bread, but it is equally good as a dip or accompaniment to main meals.

INGREDIENTS

1 (8-ounce) package fresh baby spinach

handful of celery leaves

3 tablespoons olive oil

2–3 garlic cloves, crushed

1 teaspoon cumin seeds

6–8 ripe black olives, pitted and finely chopped

1 large bunch of fresh flat-leaf parsley leaves, finely chopped

1 large bunch of cilantro leaves, finely chopped

1 teaspoon smoked paprika

juice of ½ lemon

salt and pepper

toasted flat bread or crusty bread and ripe black olives, to serve

1. Place the spinach and celery leaves in a steamer and steam until tender. Refresh the leaves under cold running water, drain well, and squeeze out the excess water. Place the steamed leaves on a wooden cutting board and chop to a pulp.

2. Heat 2 tablespoons of the oil in a heavy casserole dish. Add the garlic and cumin seeds, then cook over medium heat for 1–2 minutes, stirring, until they emit a nutty aroma. Stir in the olives with the parsley and cilantro, then add the paprika.

3. Toss in the pulped spinach and celery and cook over low heat, stirring occasionally, for 10 minutes, until the mixture is smooth and compact. Season with salt and pepper and let cool.

4. Transfer the mixture to a bowl and bind with the remaining oil and the lemon juice. Serve with toasted flat bread or crusty bread and olives.

Couscous Salad with Roasted Butternut Squash

 SERVES 4

PREP TIME:
10 minutes

COOKING TIME:
30–40 minutes

nutritional information per serving	370 cal, 13g fat, 2g sat fat, 19g total sugars, trace salt

Couscous is a Mediterranean favorite and can be cooked in many ways, including this Moroccan-inspired salad.

INGREDIENTS

2 tablespoons honey

¼ cup olive oil

1 butternut squash, peeled, seeded, and cut into ¾-inch chunks

1¼ cups couscous

1¾ cups low-sodium vegetable stock

½ cucumber, diced

1 zucchini, diced

1 red bell pepper, seeded and diced

juice of ½ lemon

2 tablespoons chopped fresh parsley

salt and pepper

1. Preheat the oven to 375°F. Mix half the honey with 1 tablespoon of the oil in a large bowl, add the squash, and toss well to coat. Transfer to a roasting pan and roast in the preheated oven for 30–40 minutes, until soft and golden.

2. Meanwhile, put the couscous in a heatproof bowl. Heat the stock in a saucepan and pour it over the couscous, cover, and let stand for 3 minutes. Add 1 tablespoon of the remaining oil and fork through, then stir in the diced cucumber, zucchini, and red bell pepper. Replace the lid and keep warm.

3. Whisk the remaining honey and oil with the lemon juice in a bowl and season with salt and pepper. Stir the mixture through the couscous.

4. To serve, top the couscous with the roasted squash and sprinkle with the parsley.

1

2

2

Crunchy Mango & Beansprout Salad *118*

Avocado Salad with Lime Dressing *120*

Couscous Salad with Roasted Butternut Squash *122*

Greek Salad Bread Bowl *124*

Broiled Cheese Kabobs on Fennel & White Bean Salad *126*

Sweet & Sour Noodles *128*

Spicy Chickpeas *130*

Thai Tofu Cakes with Chile Dip *132*

Spicy Bok Choy with Sesame Sauce *134*

Tomato Rice *136*

Stir-Fried Broccoli *138*

Caramelized Apple & Blue Cheese Salad *140*

Vegetable & Hazelnut Loaf *142*

Pepper & Basil Stacks *144*

Creamy Mushroom Crepes *146*

Potato & Chive Pancakes *148*

Crispy Crepes with Ratatouille *150*

Eggplant, Red Pepper & Basil Crepe Rolls *152*

Feta & Spinach Mini Tarts *154*

Spinach Pie *156*

Glazed Beet & Egg Sourdough Bread *158*

Tomato Tart *160*

Risotto with Asparagus & Walnuts *162*

Spicy Polenta with Poached Eggs *164*

Broiled Cheese Kabobs on Fennel & White Bean Salad

 SERVES 4

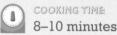 PREP TIME: 10 minutes

COOKING TIME: 8–10 minutes

nutritional information per serving	338 cal, 24g fat, 10g sat fat, 2.5g total sugars, 1.2g salt

Mozzarella is the perfect choice for mini kabobs because it keeps its shape when broiled.

INGREDIENTS

7 ounces vegetarian mozzarella or Muenster cheese

1 garlic clove, crushed

1 fennel bulb, thinly sliced

1 small red onion, thinly sliced

1 (15-ounce) can cannellini beans, drained

1–2 tablespoons balsamic vinegar, to serve

dressing

finely grated rind and juice of 1 lemon

3 tablespoons chopped fresh flat-leaf parsley

¼ cup olive oil

salt and pepper

1. Soak four wooden skewers in water for 30 minutes to prevent them from charring. Preheat the broiler to high. For the dressing, mix together the lemon rind and juice, parsley, and oil and season with salt and pepper.

2. Cut the cheese into ¾-inch cubes, thread onto the four presoaked wooden skewers, and brush with half the dressing.

3. Cook the skewers under the preheated broiler for 6–8 minutes, turning once, until golden.

4. Heat the remaining dressing and the garlic in a small saucepan until boiling. Combine with the fennel, onion, and beans.

5. Serve the skewers with the salad, sprinkled with a little balsamic vinegar.

2

3
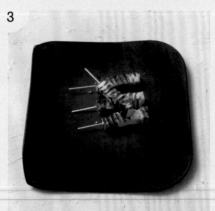

4

SOMETHING DIFFERENT
If fennel is not in
season, replace it with
thinly sliced celery
stalks and use the
leafy tops as garnish.

Sweet & Sour Noodles

 SERVES 4   PREP TIME: 10 minutes   COOKING TIME: 12–15 minutes

nutritional information per serving	254 cal, 6g fat, 1.5g sat fat, 14g total sugars, 2.3g salt

Increase the protein content by adding some toasted cashew nuts, cubed firm tofu, cooked black beans, or toasted mixed seeds with the noodles at step 3.

INGREDIENTS

5 ounces dried medium egg noodles

2 teaspoons sunflower oil

1 large red bell pepper, seeded and thinly sliced

1½ cups bean sprouts

5 scallions, thinly sliced

3 tablespoons Chinese rice wine or dry sherry

salt

sauce

3 tablespoons light soy sauce

2 tablespoons honey

2 tablespoons tomato paste

2 teaspoons cornstarch

2 teaspoons sesame oil

½ cup vegetable stock

1. Bring a large saucepan of lightly salted water to a boil. Add the noodles, bring back to a boil, and cook according to the package directions, until tender but still firm to the bite. Drain.

2. To make the sauce, put the soy sauce, honey, tomato paste, cornstarch, and sesame oil into a small bowl and mix together until smooth, then stir in the stock.

3. Heat the sunflower oil in a wok or large, heavy skillet. Add the red bell pepper and stir-fry for 4 minutes, until soft. Add the bean sprouts and stir-fry for 1 minute. Add the noodles and scallions, then pour the wine and sauce over the the vegetables and noodles. Toss together over the heat for 1–2 minutes, until the sauce is bubbling and thickened and the noodles are heated all the way through. Serve immediately.

Spicy Chickpeas

 SERVES 4    PREP TIME: 10 minutes   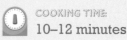 COOKING TIME: 10–12 minutes

nutritional information per serving	190 cal, 2.2g fat, 0.2g sat fat, 10g total sugars, 0.4g salt

This traditional Indian dish goes really well with plain boiled rice and a cucumber raita.

INGREDIENTS

1 (15-ounce) can chickpeas, drained and rinsed

2 Yukon gold or white round potatoes, peeled and diced

2 tablespoons tamarind paste

⅓ cup water

1 teaspoon chili powder

2 teaspoons sugar

1 onion, chopped

salt

to garnish
1 tomato, sliced

2 fresh green chiles, chopped

2–3 tablespoons chopped cilantro

1. Place the drained and rinsed chickpeas in a large bowl.

2. Put the potatoes in a saucepan of water and boil for 10–12 minutes, or until cooked all the way through. Drain and set aside.

3. Mix together the tamarind paste and water in a small bowl.

4. Add the chili powder, sugar, and 1 teaspoon of salt to the tamarind paste mixture and mix together. Pour the mixture over the chickpeas.

5. Add the onion and the diced potatoes, then stir to mix.

6. Transfer to a serving bowl and garnish with tomato, chiles, and chopped cilantro. Serve immediately.

2

5

5

COOK'S NOTE

Tamarind paste is sold in slabs and can be found in Asian grocery stores or online. It has a unique, sour flavor, which cannot be substituted.

Thai Tofu Cakes with Chile Dip

 SERVES 4   PREP TIME: 10 minutes plus chilling   COOKING TIME: 10–12 minutes

nutritional information per serving	226 cal, 10g fat, 1.5g sat fat, 5g total sugars, 0.7g salt

Similar to a fish cake, this Thai favorite would also make a great appetizer or snack with drinks.

INGREDIENTS

2 cups coarsely grated firm tofu

1 lemongrass stalk, finely chopped

2 garlic cloves, chopped

1-inch piece fresh ginger, grated

2 kaffir lime leaves, finely chopped (optional)

2 shallots, finely chopped

2 fresh red chiles, seeded and finely chopped

¼ cup chopped cilantro

¾ cup all-purpose flour, plus extra for dusting

½ teaspoon salt

vegetable oil, for cooking

chile dip

3 tablespoons white distilled vinegar

2 scallions, finely sliced

1 tablespoon sugar

2 fresh chiles, chopped

2 tablespoons chopped cilantro

pinch of salt

1. To make the chile dip, mix together all the ingredients in a small serving bowl and set aside.

2. Mix the tofu with the lemongrass, garlic, ginger, lime leaves, if using, shallots, chiles, and cilantro in a mixing bowl. Stir in the flour and salt to make a coarse, sticky paste. Cover and chill in the refrigerator for 1 hour to let the mixture become slightly firm.

3. Form the mixture into eight walnut-size balls and, using floured hands, flatten into circles. Heat enough oil to cover the bottom of a large, heavy skillet over medium heat. Cook the cakes in two batches, turning halfway through, for 4–6 minutes, or until golden brown. Drain on paper towels and serve warm with the chile dip.

Spicy Bok Choy
with Sesame Sauce

 SERVES 4   PREP TIME: 10 minutes   COOKING TIME: 8–10 minutes

nutritional information per serving	163 cal, 14g fat, 2g sat fat, 4.5g total sugars, 1.7g salt

There are various spellings of bok choy, a member of the cabbage family. Choose the smaller, more tender ones with perky leaves and unblemished stems.

INGREDIENTS

2 teaspoons peanut oil or vegetable oil

1 red chile, seeded and thinly sliced

1 garlic clove, thinly sliced

5 small bok choys, quartered

½ cup vegetable stock

sauce

2½ tablespoons sesame seeds

2 tablespoons dark soy sauce

2 teaspoons light brown sugar

1 garlic clove, crushed

3 tablespoons sesame oil

1. For the sesame sauce, toast the sesame seeds in a dry skillet set over medium heat, stirring until lightly browned. Remove from the heat and cool slightly. Transfer to a mortar and pestle. Add the soy sauce, sugar, and crushed garlic and pound to a coarse paste. Stir in the sesame oil.

2. Heat the peanut oil in a wok or large skillet. Add the chile and sliced garlic and stir-fry for 20–30 seconds. Add the bok choy and stir-fry for 5 minutes, adding the stock a little at a time to prevent sticking.

3. Transfer the bok choy to a warm dish, drizzle the sesame sauce over the top, and serve immediately.

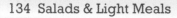

COOK'S NOTE

This sesame sauce recipe is a great standby to keep in the refrigerator; it is excellent poured over most steamed vegetables.

Tomato Rice

SERVES 4 | **PREP TIME:** 10 minutes | **COOKING TIME:** 25–30 minutes

nutritional information per serving	210 cal, 1g fat, 0.1g sat fat, 4g total sugars, trace salt

Colorful tomato-flavored rice is great for serving to the family with a wide selection of main dishes.

INGREDIENTS

1 onion, chopped

6 plum tomatoes, peeled, seeded, and chopped

1 cup vegetable stock

1 cup long-grain rice

salt and pepper

1. Put the onion and tomatoes in a food processor and process to a smooth puree. Scrape the puree into a saucepan, pour in the stock, and bring to a boil over medium heat, stirring occasionally.

2. Add the rice and stir once, then reduce the heat, cover, and simmer for 20–25 minutes, until all the liquid has been absorbed and the rice is tender. Season with salt and pepper and serve immediately.

SOMETHING
DIFFERENT
You could use
firm, ripe pears
instead of
apples, and
toasted pine
nuts instead
of walnuts.

Vegetable & Hazelnut Loaf

 MAKES
1 loaf

 PREP TIME:
15 minutes

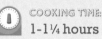 COOKING TIME:
1–1¼ hours

nutritional information per loaf	1,666 cal, 108g fat, 10g sat fat, 34g total sugars, 5.6g salt

A really popular meatless loaf that's also versatile. Delicious served hot with a tomato sauce or cold with salad.

INGREDIENTS

2 tablespoons sunflower oil, plus extra for oiling

1 onion, chopped

1 garlic clove, finely chopped

2 celery stalks, chopped

1 tablespoon all-purpose flour

1 cup tomato puree

2½ cups fresh whole-wheat bread crumbs

2 carrots, peeled and shredded

1 cup toasted hazelnuts, ground

1 tablespoon dark soy sauce

2 tablespoons chopped cilantro

1 egg, lightly beaten

salt and pepper

mixed red and green lettuce, to serve

1. Preheat the oven to 350°F. Oil and line an 8½-inch loaf pan. Heat the oil in a heavy skillet. Add the onion and cook over medium heat, stirring frequently, for 5 minutes, or until softened. Add the garlic and celery and cook, stirring frequently, for 5 minutes. Add the flour and cook, stirring, for 1 minute. Gradually stir in the tomato puree and cook, stirring continuously, until thickened. Remove the skillet from the heat.

2. Place the bread crumbs, carrots, ground hazelnuts, soy sauce, and cilantro in a bowl. Add the tomato mixture and stir well. Cool slightly, then beat in the egg and season with salt and pepper.

3. Spoon the mixture into the prepared pan and smooth the surface. Cover with aluminum foil and bake in the preheated oven for 1 hour. If serving hot, invert the loaf onto a warm serving dish, or alternatively, cool the loaf in the pan before inverting.

Pepper & Basil Stacks

 SERVES 4   PREP TIME: 15 minutes plus chilling   COOKING TIME: No cooking

nutritional information per serving | 62 cal, 1.5g fat, 0.5g sat fat, 10g total sugars, trace salt

A really attractive way to serve layered vegetables. Serve with warm garlic bread as a great appetizer to start off a special meal.

INGREDIENTS

1 teaspoon olive oil

2 shallots, finely chopped

2 garlic cloves, crushed

2 red bell peppers, peeled, seeded, and sliced into strips

1 orange bell pepper, peeled, seeded, and sliced into strips

4 tomatoes, thinly sliced

2 tablespoons shredded fresh basil, plus extra leaves to garnish

pepper

1. Lightly brush four ramekins (individual ceramic dishes) with the oil. Mix together the shallots and garlic in a bowl and season with pepper.

2. Layer the red and orange bell peppers with the tomatoes in the prepared ramekins, sprinkling each layer with the shallot mixture and shredded basil. When all the ingredients have been added, cover lightly with plastic wrap or parchment paper. Weigh down using small weights and let stand in the refrigerator for at least 6 hours, or preferably overnight.

3. When ready to serve, remove the weights and carefully run a knife around the edges. Invert onto serving plates and serve garnished with basil leaves.

1

2

3

SOMETHING DIFFERENT

If you don't have individual dishes, layer the vegetables in a larger dish. To serve, use a sharp knife to slice in wedges.

Creamy Mushroom Crepes

 SERVES 2

PREP TIME:
10 minutes

COOKING TIME:
5 minutes

nutritional information per serving	562 cal, 39g fat, 15g sat fat, 8g total sugars, 0.6g salt

This really quick mushroom filling makes a perfect partner for whole-wheat crepes.

INGREDIENTS

¼ cup light olive oil

4 cups sliced cremini mushrooms

1 teaspoon dried thyme or 2 teaspoons fresh thyme leaves

2 tablespoons chopped fresh flat-leaf parsley

1 cup reduced-fat crème fraîche

⅔ cup whole-wheat flour

1 teaspoon baking powder

1 egg

1 cup low-fat milk

salt and pepper

1. Heat 2 tablespoons of the oil in a skillet. Add the mushrooms, thyme, and half the parsley. Season with salt and pepper and cook over high heat for 2 minutes. Stir in the crème fraîche.

2. Beat together the flour, baking powder, egg, and milk in a bowl and season with salt and pepper. Heat ½ teaspoon of the remaining oil in an 8-inch nonstick skillet until hot. Add one-quarter of the batter, tilting the skillet to cover the bottom. Cook over high heat for 30 seconds, then flip the crepe and cook for an additional minute. Slide it onto a warm plate. Repeat to make another three crepes.

3. Spoon one-quarter of the mushroom mixture into the center of each crepe and fold over. Sprinkle with the remaining parsley and serve.

1   2   3

BE PREPARED

Make and fill the crepes in advance and arrange in an ovenproof dish. Cover with aluminum foil and reheat in a medium-hot oven until the filling is bubbling.

Potato & Chive Pancakes

 SERVES 4    PREP TIME: 10 minutes   COOKING TIME: 8–10 minutes

nutritional information per serving	300 cal, 12g fat, 3g sat fat, 4g total sugars, 1g salt

Delicate pancakes made with shredded potato and flavored with chives make a great light lunch.

INGREDIENTS

1¼ cups all-purpose white flour

1½ teaspoons baking powder

1 cup whole milk

1 extra-large egg

2 tablespoons sunflower oil, plus extra for greasing

2 potatoes

2 tablespoons snipped chives

1 tablespoon whole-grain mustard

salt and pepper

Greek-style yogurt or sour cream, to serve

1. Sift the flour, baking powder, and a pinch of salt into a bowl. Add the milk, egg, and oil and beat to a smooth batter.

2. Peel the potatoes and coarsely shred them, then place in a colander or strainer and sprinkle with salt. Let stand for 5 minutes, then press out as much liquid as possible. Stir the shredded potato into the batter with the chives and mustard and season with pepper.

3. Lightly grease a flat griddle pan or skillet and heat over medium heat. Spoon tablespoons of batter onto the pan and cook until bubbles appear on the surface.

4. Turn over with a spatula and cook the other side until golden brown. Repeat this process using the remaining batter, while keeping the cooked pancakes warm.

5. Serve immediately, with a spoonful of yogurt.

COOK'S TIP

Best served freshly made, keep cooked pancakes warm on a baking sheet in a moderate oven while cooking the remainder.

Crispy Crepes with Ratatouille

 SERVES 4

PREP TIME:
15 minutes
plus standing

COOKING TIME:
1 hour

nutritional information per serving	410 cal, 20g fat, 4g sat fat, 9g total sugars, 0.8g salt

A great family dish, just serve with a crisp green salad and crusty bread.

INGREDIENTS

⅔ cup all-purpose white flour
⅔ cup whole-wheat flour
pinch of salt
1 cup whole milk
½ cup water
1 extra-large egg
2 tablespoons olive oil
sunflower oil, for greasing and brushing
¼ cup dry whole-wheat bread crumbs

filling
3 tablespoons olive oil
1 red onion, diced
1 large eggplant, diced
1 garlic clove, crushed
1 large zucchini, diced
1 (14-ounce) can diced tomatoes
2 tablespoons chopped fresh oregano
salt and pepper

1. For the filling, heat the oil in a large skillet over medium heat, add the onion and eggplant, and sauté until golden. Add the garlic, zucchini, tomatoes, and oregano and season with salt and pepper. Cover and simmer for 25–30 minutes, or until tender.

2. Meanwhile, sift the two types of flour and the salt into a bowl, tipping in any bran left in the sifter. Add the milk, water, egg, and olive oil and beat to a smooth, bubbly batter. Let stand for 15 minutes.

3. Grease an 8-inch skillet and heat over medium heat. Pour in enough batter to just cover the skillet, swirling to cover in a thin, even layer. Cook until the underside is golden, then flip or turn with a spatula and cook the other side until golden.

4. Repeat this process using the remaining batter. Interleave the cooked crepes with paper towels and keep warm.

5. Preheat the oven to 400°F and grease a wide, ovenproof dish.

6. Spoon the filling onto one side of each crepe and fold over the other side. Arrange in the prepared dish in one layer, brush with oil, and sprinkle with bread crumbs. Bake for 25–30 minutes, until golden. Serve immediately.

Eggplant, Red Pepper & Basil Crepe Rolls

 SERVES 4

 PREP TIME:
15 minutes
plus standing

COOKING TIME:
15 minutes

nutritional information per serving	560 cal, 41g fat, 22g sat fat, 9g total sugars, 0.6g salt

Serve these vegetable and cheese rolls wrapped in paper napkins for fast food at home.

INGREDIENTS

1¼ cups all-purpose white flour
pinch of salt
1 cup whole milk
½ cup water
1 extra-large egg
2 tablespoons olive oil
sunflower oil, for greasing

filling

2 large eggplants
olive oil, for brushing
2 large red bell peppers, halved and seeded
1 cup vegetarian cream cheese
handful of fresh basil leaves
salt and pepper

1. For the filling, slice the eggplants lengthwise into ¼-inch thick slices, sprinkle with salt, and let drain for about 20 minutes. Rinse and dry.

2. Preheat the broiler to high. Arrange the eggplant slices on a baking sheet in a single layer, brush with olive oil, and broil until golden, turning once. Arrange the red bell peppers, cut side down, on a baking sheet in a single layer and broil until blackened. Remove the skins and slice.

3. Sift the flour and salt into a bowl. Add the milk, water, egg, and oil and beat to a smooth, bubbly batter. Let stand for 15 minutes.

4. Lightly grease an 8-inch skillet and heat over medium heat. Pour in enough batter to just cover the skillet, swirling to cover in a thin, even layer. Cook until the underside is golden, then flip or turn with a spatula and cook the other side until golden brown.

5. Repeat this process using the remaining batter. Interleave the cooked crepes with paper towels and keep warm.

6. Arrange the pancakes in pairs, slightly overlapping. Spread with cheese, top with the eggplants, red bell peppers, and basil, and season with salt and pepper. Roll up firmly from one short side. Cut in half diagonally and serve immediately.

Feta & Spinach Mini Tarts

 MAKES 6

 PREP TIME:
15 minutes
plus chilling

 COOKING TIME:
25 minutes

nutritional information per tartlet	478 cal, 41g fat, 22g sat fat, 2g total sugars, 1.2g salt

These mini tarts are perfect for a picnic alongside celery, carrot sticks, and a spicy salsa for dipping.

INGREDIENTS

pastry dough
1 cup all-purpose flour, plus extra for dusting

pinch of salt

5½ tablespoons cold butter, cut into pieces, plus extra for greasing

½ teaspoon ground nutmeg

1–2 tablespoons cold water

filling
9 ounces baby spinach

2 tablespoons butter

⅔ cup heavy cream

3 egg yolks

4 ounces vegetarian feta cheese

⅓ cup pine nuts

salt and pepper

1. Grease six 3½-inch loose-bottom round tart pans. Sift the flour and salt into a food processor, add the butter, and process until the mixture resembles fine bread crumbs. Transfer the mixture to a large bowl and add the nutmeg and enough cold water to bring the dough together.

2. Invert the dough onto a floured surface and divide into six equal pieces. Roll each piece to fit the tart pans. Carefully fit each piece of dough in its pan and press well to fit. Roll the rolling pin over the pan to neaten the edges and trim the excess dough. Cut out six pieces of parchment paper and fit a piece into each tart, fill with pie weights or dried beans, and chill in the refrigerator for 30 minutes.

3. Preheat the oven to 400°F. Bake the tart shells in the preheated oven for 10 minutes, then remove the weights and paper.

4. Blanch the spinach in boiling water for just 1 minute, then drain and press to squeeze all the water out. Chop the spinach. Melt the butter in a skillet, add the spinach, and cook gently to evaporate any remaining liquid. Season well with salt and pepper. Stir in the cream and egg yolks. Crumble the cheese and divide among the tarts, top with the spinach mixture, and bake for 10 minutes. Scatter the pine nuts over the mini tarts and cook for an additional 5 minutes.

5. Let rest in the tart pans for 5 minutes, then gently remove the mini tarts from the pan and let cool on a wire rack. Serve warm or cold.

Spinach Pie

 SERVES 8

 PREP TIME:
30 minutes
plus chilling

COOKING TIME:
60 minutes

nutritional information per serving	483 cal, 32g fat, 17g sat fat, 3g total sugars, 1.1g salt

The perfect combination of spinach and ricotta encased in crispy, flaky pastry.

INGREDIENTS

pastry dough
2¾ cups all-purpose flour, plus extra for dusting

pinch of salt

1½ sticks butter, diced, plus extra for greasing

2 egg yolks

⅓ cup ice-cold water

filling
3 cups thawed, frozen spinach (about 1 pound)

2 tablespoons olive oil

1 large onion, chopped

2 garlic cloves, finely chopped

2 eggs, lightly beaten

8 ounces vegetarian ricotta cheese

½ cup freshly grated vegetarian Parmesan-style cheese

pinch of freshly grated nutmeg

salt and pepper

1. To make the dough, sift the flour with the salt into a bowl. Add the butter and rub into the flour with your fingertips until the mixture resembles fine bread crumbs. Beat the egg yolks with the water in a small bowl. Sprinkle the liquid over the flour mixture and combine with a rubber spatula to form a dough. Shape into a ball, wrap in aluminum foil, and chill in the refrigerator for 30 minutes.

2. Meanwhile, preheat the oven to 400°F. Lightly grease a 9-inch loose-bottom tart pan. To make the filling, drain the spinach and squeeze out as much moisture as possible. Heat the oil in a large, heavy skillet over medium heat. Add the onion and cook, stirring frequently, for 5 minutes, or until softened. Add the garlic and spinach and cook, stirring occasionally, for 10 minutes. Remove from the heat and let cool slightly, then beat in the eggs (reserving a little for glazing), ricotta, and grated cheese. Season with salt and pepper and nutmeg.

3. Roll out two-thirds of the dough on a lightly floured work surface and use to line the pan. Spoon in the spinach mixture, spreading it evenly over the bottom.

4. Roll out the remaining dough on a lightly floured surface and cut into ¼-inch strips. Arrange the strips in a lattice pattern on top of the tart, pressing the ends securely to seal. Trim any excess dough. Brush with the egg to glaze and bake in the preheated oven for 45 minutes, or until golden brown. Transfer to a wire rack to cool slightly before removing from the pan.

3

4

Glazed Beet & Egg Sourdough Bread

 SERVES 4   PREP TIME: 10 minutes   COOKING TIME: 12–15 minutes

nutritional information per serving	404 cal, 24g fat, 4g sat fat, 14g total sugars, 1.4g salt

Try this traditional combination of ruby red beets and chopped egg served on sourdough bread for a great lunch dish.

INGREDIENTS

4 eggs

8 cooked beetroot (fresh or vacuum-packed without vinegar)

2 teaspoons sugar

5 teaspoons cider vinegar

4 slices sourdough bread (from a long oval loaf)

⅓ cup olive oil

1 tablespoon Dijon mustard

3 tablespoons chopped fresh dill, plus extra sprigs to garnish

salt and pepper

1. Preheat the broiler to medium–high setting. Boil the eggs in a saucepan of boiling water for 5 minutes, then drain, shell, and chop them. Set aside. Dice the beets finely and place in a small bowl. Mix in half the sugar, 1 teaspoon of the cider vinegar, and season with salt and pepper.

2. Brush the bread with a little olive oil and toast on one side on the rack in the broiler pan for 2–3 minutes, until crisp and golden.

3. Meanwhile, trickle 1 teaspoon of the remaining oil over the beets. Beat together the remaining cider vinegar, mustard, and remaining sugar and season with salt and pepper. Gradually beat in the remaining oil to make a thick dressing. Stir in the dill and taste for seasoning—it should be sweet and mustardy, with a sharpness—add more sugar or vinegar, if you desire.

4. Turn over the bread and top with the beets after first stirring them, covering the slices right up to the crusts. Glaze the beets under the broiler for 2–3 minutes, until browned in places.

5. Cut the slices in half or quarters and top with egg. Drizzle with a little dressing, garnish with the dill sprigs, and serve immediately.

3

4

Tomato Tart

 SERVES 4    PREP TIME: 15 minutes   COOKING TIME: 25–30 minutes

nutritional information per serving	557 cal, 35g fat, 22g sat fat, 9g total sugars, 0.7g salt

An inspirational twist on the French classic dessert made with apples.

INGREDIENTS

2 tablespoons butter
1 tablespoon sugar
3½ cups halved cherry tomatoes
1 garlic clove, crushed
2 teaspoons white wine vinegar
salt and pepper

pastry dough
2 cups all-purpose flour, sifted
pinch of salt
1¼ sticks butter
1 tablespoon chopped oregano, plus extra to garnish
⅓ cup cold water

1. Preheat the oven to 400°F. Melt the butter in a heavy skillet. Add the sugar and stir over high heat until just turning golden brown.

2. Remove from the heat and quickly add the tomatoes, garlic, and white wine vinegar, stirring to coat evenly. Season with salt and pepper. Transfer the tomatoes to a 9-inch cake pan, spreading evenly.

3. For the pastry dough, place the flour, salt, butter, and oregano in a food processor and process until the mixture resembles fine bread crumbs. Add just enough water to bind to a soft, but not sticky, dough.

4. Roll out the dough to a 10-inch circle and place it over the tomatoes, tucking in the edges. Pierce with a fork to let out steam.

5. Bake in the preheated oven for 25–30 minutes, until firm and golden. Rest for 2–3 minutes, then run a knife around the edge and invert onto a warm serving plate. Sprinkle the tart with chopped oregano and serve warm.

Risotto with Asparagus & Walnuts

 SERVES 4   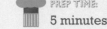 PREP TIME: 5 minutes   COOKING TIME: 20–25 minutes

nutritional information per serving	550 cal, 20g fat, 4g sat fat, 2.5g total sugars, trace salt

Welcome spring with this classic rice dish and use the freshest asparagus you can find.

INGREDIENTS

1 tablespoon butter

3 tablespoons olive oil

1 small onion, finely chopped

1¾ cups risotto rice

⅔ cup dry white wine

6½ cups hot vegetable stock

7 ounces asparagus tips, cut into 2½-inch lengths

⅓ cup chopped walnuts

grated rind of 1 lemon

salt and pepper

walnut oil, to serve (optional)

strips of lemon zest, to garnish

1. Heat the butter and olive oil in a large saucepan and sauté the onion, stirring, for 3–4 minutes, until softened. Add the rice and stir over medium heat for 1 minute, without browning. Add the wine and boil rapidly, stirring, until almost all the wine has evaporated.

2. Stir the stock into the pan a ladleful at a time, allowing each ladleful to be absorbed before adding another one. After 10 minutes, add the asparagus and continue cooking, adding more stock when necessary. After an additional 5 minutes, test a grain of rice—it should be "al dente," or firm to the bite.

3. Stir in the walnuts and lemon rind, then adjust the seasoning, adding salt and pepper. Remove from the heat and drizzle with a little walnut oil, if using, stirring in lightly. Serve the risotto immediately, garnished with strips of lemon zest.

Spicy Polenta with Poached Eggs

 SERVES 4

 PREP TIME:
10 minutes
plus cooling

COOKING TIME:
11–15 minutes

nutritional information per serving	414 cal, 24g fat, 11g sat fat, 1g total sugars, 1g salt

To use the polenta scraps, chop coarsely, place in a shallow ovenproof dish, brush with melted butter, and broil for 3 minutes. Serve as an unusual side dish.

INGREDIENTS

oil, for oiling

2½ cups water

1 cup polenta or cornmeal

1 cup freshly grated vegetarian Parmesan-style cheese

3 tablespoons butter

½–1 red chile, seeded and finely chopped

7 cups baby spinach leaves, or a mixture of baby spinach leaves and arugula leaves

2 teaspoons white wine vinegar

4 extra-large eggs

salt and pepper

1. Lightly oil an 7-inch square cake pan. Bring the water to a boil in a saucepan. Add the polenta in a thin stream and cook, stirring, over medium–low heat for 3 minutes, until thick. Stir in ⅔ cup of the cheese, 2 tablespoons of the butter, and the chile. Working quickly, transfer to the prepared pan and level the surface. Set aside for 30 minutes, until cool and firm, then cut out 4 circles with a 3½-inch pastry cutter and transfer to a baking sheet.

2. Preheat the broiler to high. Wash the spinach and place in a large saucepan with the water clinging to the leaves. Cover and cook for 2–3 minutes, until wilted, then squeeze out the excess water between two plates. Return to the pan.

3. Sprinkle the polenta circles with the remaining cheese, place under the preheated broiler, and cook for 3 minutes, until brown and bubbling on the top. Keep warm. Meanwhile, add the remaining butter to the spinach, season with salt and pepper, and heat all the way through.

4. Fill a saucepan halfway with water, add the vinegar, and bring to simmering point. Crack the eggs into cups and slide gently into the water. Poach over low heat, without letting the water boil, for 3 minutes, until the whites are firm and the yolk is still soft. Scoop out with a slotted spoon and drain briefly on paper towels.

5. To serve, place the polenta circles on four warm plates and divide the spinach among them. Top with the eggs and sprinkle with a little salt and pepper. Serve immediately.

Chile Broccoli Pasta *168*

Grilled Zucchini & Feta Pizza *170*

Spicy Eggplant & Chickpea Penne *172*

Spaghetti with Lentil & Tomato Sauce *174*

Rigatoni with Roasted Zucchini, Tomato & Cheese Sauce *176*

Sichuan Mixed Vegetables *178*

Satay Noodles *180*

Teriyaki Tofu Stir-Fry *182*

New Potato, Feta & Herb Frittata *184*

Caponata *186*

Bean & Vegetable Chili *188*

Pasta with Two Cheeses & Walnuts *190*

Mediterranean Vegetables with Feta & Olives *192*

Spiced Vegetables *194*

Red Curry with Mixed Greens *196*

Quinoa with Roasted Vegetables *198*

Stir-Fried Rice with Green Vegetables *200*

Bean Burgers *202*

Leek, Herb & Mushroom Risotto *204*

Ricotta, Spinach & Pine Nut Pizza *206*

Smoky Mushroom & Herb Burgers *208*

Mixed Nut Loaf *210*

Mushroom & Onion Quiche *212*

Chinese Greens Curry *214*

Dinners

Chile Broccoli Pasta

 SERVES 4    PREP TIME: 5 minutes   COOKING TIME: 10–15 minutes

nutritional information per serving	300 cal, 11g fat, 1.5g sat fat, 3g total sugars, trace salt

A dish made with these ingredients can't fail—they just seem right together. Good for serving to a crowd.

INGREDIENTS

8 ounces dried penne or macaroni

3 cups broccoli florets

¼ cup extra virgin olive oil

2 large garlic cloves, chopped

2 fresh red chiles, seeded and diced

8 cherry tomatoes

handful of fresh basil leaves, to garnish

salt

1. Bring a large saucepan of lightly salted water to a boil. Add the pasta, return to a boil, and cook according to the package directions, until tender but still firm to the bite. Drain the pasta, refresh under cold running water, and drain again. Set aside.

2. Bring a separate saucepan of lightly salted water to a boil, add the broccoli, and cook for 5 minutes. Drain, refresh under cold running water, and drain again.

3. Heat the oil in a large, heavy skillet over high heat. Add the garlic, chiles, and tomatoes and cook, stirring continuously, for 1 minute.

4. Add the broccoli and mix well. Cook for 2 minutes, stirring, to heat all the way through. Add the pasta and mix well again. Cook for an additional minute. Transfer the pasta to a large, warm serving bowl and serve immediately, garnished with basil leaves.

1

2

4

COOK'S NOTE

Don't be tempted to chop fresh basil with a knife–it will turn black. Use small leaves or tear larger ones into pieces.

Grilled Zucchini
& Feta Pizza

 MAKES
2 pizzas

 PREP TIME:
20 minutes
plus rising

COOKING TIME:
15–20 minutes

nutritional information per pizza	996 cal, 42g fat, 20g sat fat, 10g total sugars, 8.6g salt

However easy it is to order a pizza, you can't beat the taste and texture of the dough when you make it yourself.

INGREDIENTS

basic pizza dough
2¼ cups white bread flour, plus extra for dusting

1 teaspoon active dry yeast

1½ teaspoons salt

¾ cup lukewarm water

1 tablespoon olive oil, plus extra for kneading

topping
1 tablespoon olive oil

1 garlic clove, crushed

1 large zucchini, sliced lengthwise

¾ cup prepared tomato-based pizza sauce

1⅓ cups crumbled, drained vegetarian feta cheese

salt and pepper

fresh mint leaves, coarsely torn, to garnish

1. Sift the flour into a mixing bowl and add the yeast and salt, making a small well in the center. Mix together the water and oil, add to the dry ingredients, and, using a rubber spatula, gradually combine all the ingredients to make a sticky dough.

2. Lightly flour the work surface and your hands and knead the dough for about 10 minutes, until it is smooth and elastic.

3. Cover the dough with some lightly oiled plastic wrap or a damp dish towel and let rise for about an hour, or until it has doubled in size.

4. Preheat the oven to 425°F. Punch down the dough to knock out the air and gently knead for about a minute, then divide into two balls. To roll out the dough, flatten each ball, then, using a rolling pin, roll out on a lightly floured surface, giving a quarter turn between each roll.

5. Place the pizza dough crusts on two baking sheets, using a rolling pin to transfer them from the work surface.

6. Heat the oil in a ridged grill pan over medium heat. Add the garlic and zucchini and cook over medium heat for 4–5 minutes, turning regularly, until softened and chargrilled. Remove with a slotted spoon and drain on paper towels.

7. Divide the pizza sauce between the two pizza crusts, spreading it almost to the edges. Place the zucchini slices on the pizza crusts, sprinkle with the cheese, and season with salt and pepper. Bake in the preheated oven for 10–12 minutes, or until the cheese is turning golden and the crusts are crisp underneath. Garnish with the fresh mint and serve immediately.

Spicy Eggplant & Chickpea Penne

 SERVES 4    PREP TIME: 10 minutes   COOKING TIME: 30 minutes

nutritional information per serving	428 cal, 9.5g fat, 1.3g sat fat, 11g total sugars, 0.5g salt

Made mostly from pantry ingredients, this can be whipped up quickly and your guests will love it.

INGREDIENTS

large pinch of saffron threads

2 cups hot vegetable stock

2 tablespoons olive oil

1 large onion, coarsely chopped

1 teaspoon cumin seeds, crushed

4 cups diced eggplant,

1 large red bell pepper, seeded and chopped

1 (14½-ounce) can diced tomatoes with garlic

1 teaspoon ground cinnamon

½ bunch of cilantro, leaves and stems separated and coarsely chopped

1 (15-ounce) can chickpeas, drained and rinsed

10 ounces dried penne

salt and pepper

chili sauce, to serve

1. Toast the saffron threads in a dry skillet set over medium heat for 20–30 seconds, just until they begin to give off their aroma. Place in a small bowl and crumble with your fingers. Add 2 tablespoons of the hot stock and set aside to infuse.

2. Heat the oil in a large saucepan. Add the onion and sauté for 5–6 minutes, until golden brown. Add the cumin and sauté for an additional 20–30 seconds, then stir in the eggplant, red bell pepper, tomatoes, cinnamon, cilantro stems, saffron liquid, and remaining stock. Cover and simmer for 20 minutes.

3. Add the chickpeas to the saucepan and season with salt and pepper. Simmer for an additional 5 minutes, removing the lid to reduce and thicken the sauce, if necessary.

4. Meanwhile, bring a large, heavy saucepan of lightly salted water to a boil. Add the pasta, return to a boil, and cook according to the package directions, until tender but still firm to the bite. Drain and transfer to a warm serving bowl. Add the sauce and half the cilantro leaves, then toss. Garnish with the remaining cilantro and serve immediately with the chili sauce.

Spaghetti with Lentil & Tomato Sauce

 SERVES 4

PREP TIME: 15 minutes

COOKING TIME: 45–55 minutes

nutritional information per serving	500 cal, 8g fat, 1g sat fat, 16.5g total sugars, 0.3g salt

No vegetarian kitchen should be without a recipe for this popular pasta sauce.

INGREDIENTS

1 cup dried green lentils

2 tablespoons olive oil

1 large onion, chopped

2 garlic cloves, crushed

2 carrots, chopped

2 celery stalks, chopped

1 (28-ounce) can diced tomatoes

⅔ cup vegetable stock

1 red bell pepper, seeded and chopped

2 tablespoons tomato paste

2 teaspoons finely chopped fresh rosemary

1 teaspoon dried oregano

10 ounces dried spaghetti or linguine

handful of basil leaves, torn

salt and pepper

freshly grated vegetarian Parmesan-style cheese, to serve

1. Put the lentils in a saucepan and cover with cold water. Bring to a boil and simmer for about 30 minutes, or according to the package directions, until just tender. Drain well.

2. Meanwhile, heat the oil in a large saucepan. Add the onion, garlic, carrots, and celery. Cover and cook over low heat for 5 minutes. Stir in the tomatoes, stock, red bell pepper, tomato paste, rosemary, and oregano. Cover and simmer for 20 minutes, until the sauce is thickened and the vegetables are tender. Add the lentils and cook, stirring, for an additional 5 minutes. Season with salt and pepper.

3. While the sauce is cooking, bring a large saucepan of lightly salted water to a boil. Add the spaghetti, bring back to a boil, and cook according to the package directions, until tender but still firm to the bite. Drain well, then divide the spaghetti among four warm bowls. Spoon the sauce over the pasta and sprinkle with the basil leaves. Serve immediately with the grated cheese on the side.

Rigatoni with Roasted Zucchini, Tomato & Cheese Sauce

SERVES 4   PREP TIME: 15 minutes   COOKING TIME: 30–35 minutes

nutritional information per serving	520 cal, 24g fat, 10g sat fat, 11g total sugars, 0.2g salt

With its creamy sauce and generous helping of roasted vegetables, this pasta dish will satisfy the heartiest of appetites.

INGREDIENTS

4 zucchini, coarsely chopped

2½ tablespoons olive oil

1 onion, finely chopped

1 garlic clove, crushed

1 (28-ounce) can diced tomatoes

6 sun-dried tomatoes, chopped

1 cup vegetable stock

½ teaspoon dried oregano

10 ounces dried rigatoni pasta

½ cup vegetarian mascarpone or ricotta cheese

salt and pepper

large handful of fresh basil leaves, torn into pieces

1. Preheat the oven to 400°F. Place the zucchini and 1½ tablespoons of the oil in a large ovenproof dish. Toss together and spread out in a single layer. Roast in the preheated oven for 15–20 minutes, until tender and lightly browned.

2. Meanwhile, heat the remaining oil in a saucepan. Add the onion and garlic and cook gently for 5 minutes, until soft. Add the canned tomatoes, sun-dried tomatoes, stock, and oregano. Simmer for 10 minutes, until the liquid has reduced slightly.

3. Bring a large saucepan of lightly salted water to a boil. Add the pasta, bring back to a boil, and cook according to the package directions, until tender but still firm to the bite. Drain well, then return to the pan.

4. Add the mascarpone cheese to the hot sauce and stir until melted and smooth. Season well with salt and pepper. Add to the pasta with the zucchini and the basil leaves. Toss together until the pasta is well coated in sauce. Serve immediately.

1

2

4

HEALTHY HINT

For a reduced-fat version, roast the zucchini on a nonstick baking sheet without oil and replace the cheese with vegetarian low-fat cream cheese.

Sichuan Mixed Vegetables

 SERVES 4   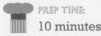 PREP TIME: 10 minutes   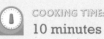 COOKING TIME: 10 minutes

nutritional information per serving | 200 cal, 18g fat, 2g sat fat, 11g total sugars, 2.2g salt

Either smooth or chunky peanut butter can be used for this recipe; it gives the dish an authentic Asian taste.

INGREDIENTS

2 tablespoons chili oil

4 garlic cloves, crushed

2-inch piece fresh ginger, grated

4 carrots, cut into thin strips

1 red bell pepper, cut into thin strips

5½ ounces shiitake mushrooms, sliced

2 cups diagonally halved snow peas

3 tablespoons soy sauce

3 tablespoons peanut butter

3½ cups bean sprouts

cooked rice, to serve

1. Heat the chili oil in a preheated wok and sauté the garlic, ginger, and carrots for 3 minutes. Add the bell pepper and stir-fry for another 2 minutes.

2. Add the mushrooms and snow peas and stir-fry for 1 minute.

3. In a small bowl, mix together the soy sauce and peanut butter until combined.

4. Using a wooden spoon, make a space in the center of the stir-fried vegetables so that the bottom of the wok is visible. Pour in the sauce and bring to a boil, stirring all the time until it starts to thicken. Add the bean sprouts and toss the vegetables to coat them thoroughly with the sauce.

5. Transfer to a warm serving dish and serve immediately with freshly cooked rice.

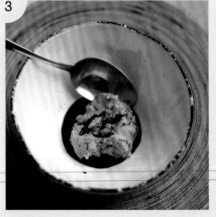

SOMETHING
DIFFERENT
This dish will
taste just as
good if served
with either egg
or rice noodles.

Satay Noodles

 SERVES 2   PREP TIME: 15 minutes    COOKING TIME: 10–15 minutes

nutritional information per serving	775 cal, 52g fat, 27g sat fat, 10g total sugars, 3.3g salt

A filling meal—and there's only one pan to clean. You can add a finely sliced chile with the garlic in step 3.

INGREDIENTS

4½ ounces dried medium egg noodles

3 ounces from block of unsweetened coconut cream, chopped, and ⅔ cup boiling water, or ⅔ cup coconut milk

2 teaspoons vegetable oil

1 large red bell pepper, seeded and thinly sliced

1 plump garlic clove, thinly sliced

1¼ cups bean sprouts

2 tablespoons dark soy sauce

⅓ cup roasted salted peanuts, coarsely chopped

3 scallions, diagonally sliced

large handful of cilantro, chopped

salt

2 lime halves, to serve

1. Bring a large saucepan of lightly salted water to a boil. Add the noodles, bring back to a boil. and cook according to the package directions, until tender but still firm to the bite. Drain.

2. Add the chopped coconut cream to a boiling water and stir until dissolved. Alternatively, skip this step if you are using coconut milk—the coconut milk won't be as rich as the coconut cream.

3. Heat the oil in a wok or large, heavy skillet. Add the bell pepper and stir-fry over high heat for 2–3 minutes, until soft. Add the garlic and stir-fry for an additional 40–60 seconds; do not let it burn.

4. Add the bean sprouts, followed by the noodles, coconut cream (or coconut milk), soy sauce, and peanuts. Reduce the heat and stir for an additional 2–3 minutes, until piping hot. Add the scallions and cilantro and toss together.

5. Divide between two warm bowls and serve immediately with the lime halves for squeezing over.

COOK'S NOTE

Look for blocks of unsweetened coconut cream at Caribbean and Asian stores.

Teriyaki Tofu Stir-Fry

 SERVES 2

PREP TIME:
15 minutes

COOKING TIME:
15 minutes

nutritional information per serving	738 cal, 25g fat, 4g sat fat, 33g total sugars, 4.6g salt

Try this method of dry-frying tofu, which makes the texture firm without adding extra calories and fat.

INGREDIENTS

5 ounces medium egg noodles

1 (8-ounce) package firm tofu, drained

2 tablespoons sunflower oil or vegetable oil

1 red bell pepper, seeded and thinly sliced

10 baby corn, diagonally sliced

3 cups choy sum or bok choy (1½-inch pieces)

salt

sauce

3 tablespoons tamari or dark soy sauce

3 tablespoons rice wine

3 tablespoons honey

1 tablespoon cornstarch

1 tablespoon finely grated fresh ginger

1–2 garlic cloves, crushed

1 cup water

1. Bring a large saucepan of lightly salted water to a boil. Add the noodles, bring back to a boil, and cook according to the package directions, until tender but still firm to the bite. Drain.

2. Meanwhile, cut the tofu into ½-inch slices and then into bite-size pieces. Pat dry on plenty of paper towels. Heat a nonstick or well-seasoned skillet over medium–low heat, then add the tofu and cook for 3 minutes, without moving the pieces around the skillet, until golden brown underneath. Turn and cook for an additional 2–3 minutes on the other side. Transfer to a plate.

3. To make the sauce, mix the tamari, rice wine, honey, cornstarch, ginger, and garlic together in a small bowl until well blended, then stir in the water. Set aside.

4. Heat the oil in a wok or large, heavy skillet. Add the bell pepper and baby corn and stir-fry for 3 minutes. Add the choy sum and stir-fry for an additional 2 minutes. Pour in the sauce and heat, stirring continuously, until it boils and thickens. Add the noodles and tofu and toss together over the heat for an additional 1–2 minutes, until heated through. Serve immediately.

New Potato, Feta & Herb Frittata

🍽 SERVES 4

👨‍🍳 PREP TIME: 10 minutes

⏱ COOKING TIME: 30–35 minutes

nutritional information per serving	273 cal, 19g fat, 8g sat fat, 1.5g total sugars, 1.5g salt

This chunky omelet is delicious cold as well as hot, so it's perfect for picnics and lunch boxes.

INGREDIENTS

6 new potatoes, scrubbed

3 cups baby spinach leaves

5 eggs

1 tablespoon chopped fresh dill, plus extra to garnish

1 tablespoon snipped fresh chives, plus extra to garnish

¾ cup crumbled, drained vegetarian feta cheese,

½ tablespoon butter

1 tablespoon olive oil

salt and pepper

1. Bring a saucepan of lightly salted water to a boil, add the potatoes, bring back to a boil, and cook for 25 minutes, until tender. Place the spinach in a colander and drain the potatoes over the top to wilt the spinach. Set aside until cool enough to handle.

2. Cut the potatoes lengthwise into ¼-in thick slices. Squeeze the excess water from the spinach leaves. Preheat the broiler to high.

3. Lightly beat together the eggs, dill, and chives. Season with pepper and add ½ cup of the cheese. Heat the butter and oil in an 8-inch skillet until melted and foaming. Add the potato slices and spinach and cook, stirring, for 1 minute. Pour the egg-and-cheese mixture over the vegetables.

4. Cook, stirring, over medium heat for 1 minute, until half set, then continue to cook for 2–3 minutes, without stirring, until set and golden brown underneath. Sprinkle the remaining cheese over the omlet, place under the preheated broiler, and cook for 2 minutes, until golden brown on top. Serve hot or cold, sprinkled with chives and dill.

1

3

4

SOMETHING DIFFERENT

This frittata is a great way of using up leftover boiled, baked, or roasted potatoes. Cut them into chunky pieces if they are too crumbly to slice.

Caponata

 SERVES 4  PREP TIME: 10 minutes plus cooling COOKING TIME: 20 minutes

nutritional information per serving	190 cal, 13g fat, 2g sat fat, 12g total sugars, 1.2g salt

A great dish from Sicily, where the exact combination of ingredients is endlessly debated. This recipe is one of the most popular.

INGREDIENTS

¼ cup olive oil
2 celery stalks, sliced
2 red onions, sliced
1 eggplant, diced
1 garlic clove, finely chopped
5 plum tomatoes, chopped
3 tablespoons red wine vinegar
1 tablespoon sugar
3 tablespoons pitted green olives
2 tablespoons capers
¼ cup chopped fresh flat-leaf parsley
salt and pepper
ciabatta bread, to serve

1. Heat half the oil in a large, heavy saucepan. Add the celery and onions and cook over low heat, stirring occasionally, for 5 minutes, until softened but not browned. Add the remaining oil and the eggplant. Cook, stirring frequently, for about 5 minutes, until the eggplant starts to brown.

2. Add the garlic, tomatoes, vinegar, and sugar and mix well. Cover the mixture with a circle of wax paper and simmer gently for about 10 minutes.

3. Remove the wax paper, stir in the olives and capers, and season with salt and pepper. Pour into a serving dish and set aside to cool to room temperature. When cool, sprinkle the parsley over the caponata and serve immediately with ciabatta bread.

1

1

2

GOES WELL WITH

When not served as a dish in its own right, Caponata can be incorporated into a multitude of recipes. Add to pasta, use to top bruschetta, or mix into scrambled eggs.

Bean & Vegetable Chili

 SERVES 4   PREP TIME: 10 minutes   COOKING TIME: 20 minutes

nutritional information per serving	180 cal, 1.5g fat, 0.2g sat fat, 14g total sugars, 1.4g salt

This must be one of the most popular dishes to serve a crowd. Be careful not to go mad with the chile—have your favorite chili sauce available so everyone can adjust the heat level to suit.

INGREDIENTS

¼ cup vegetable stock

1 onion, coarsely chopped

1 green bell pepper, seeded and finely chopped

1 red bell pepper, seeded and finely chopped

1 teaspoon finely chopped garlic

1 teaspoon finely chopped fresh ginger

2 teaspoons ground cumin

½ teaspoon chili powder

2 tablespoons tomato paste

1 (14½-ounce) can diced tomatoes

1 (15-ounce) can kidney beans, drained and rinsed

1 (15-ounce) can black-eyed peas, drained and rinsed

salt and pepper

tortilla chips, to serve

1. Heat the stock in a large saucepan, add the onion and bell peppers, and simmer for 5 minutes, or until softened.

2. Stir in the garlic, ginger, cumin, chili powder, tomato paste, and tomatoes. Season with salt and pepper and simmer for 10 minutes.

3. Stir in all the beans and simmer for an additional 5 minutes, or until heated through. Serve immediately with tortilla chips.

Pasta with Two Cheeses & Walnuts

 SERVES 4   PREP TIME: 5 minutes   COOKING TIME: 15 minutes

nutritional information per serving	838 cal, 49g fat, 20g sat fat, 5g total sugars, 0.9g salt

The perfect dish to eat curled up on the couch watching TV. Alternatively, it makes a wonderful meal for a more formal dining setting, served with a crisp salad and a glass of wine.

INGREDIENTS

12 ounces dried penne

2 cups fresh or frozen peas

⅔ cup vegetarian cream cheese with garlic and herbs

1 (6-ounce) package baby spinach leaves

1 cup diced vegetarian blue cheese

1 cup coarsely chopped walnuts

salt and pepper

1. Cook the pasta in a large saucepan of lightly salted, boiling water according to the package directions, adding the peas for the final 2 minutes. Drain, reserving ½ cup of the hot cooking liquid.

2. Return the pan to the heat. Add the reserved cooking liquid and the cream cheese. Heat, stirring, until melted and smooth.

3. Remove from the heat, then add the spinach to the pan, followed by the pasta, peas, blue cheese, and walnuts. Season with pepper and toss together, until the spinach has wilted and the cheese has started to melt. Serve immediately.

COOK'S NOTE
A splash of olive oil added to the cooking water helps prevent the pasta from sticking together.

Mediterranean Vegetables with Feta & Olives

 SERVES 4   PREP TIME: 10 minutes   COOKING TIME: 20–25 minutes

nutritional information per serving	240 cal, 12g fat, 2.5g sat fat, 11g total sugars, 0.7g salt

Let the wonderful aromas wafting from the kitchen remind you of warm evenings dining alfresco.

INGREDIENTS

1 red onion, sliced into thick rings

1 small eggplant, thickly sliced

2 large mushrooms, halved

3 red bell peppers, halved and seeded

3 plum tomatoes, peeled and diced

2 garlic cloves, minced

1 tablespoon chopped fresh flat-leaf parsley

1 teaspoon chopped fresh rosemary

1 teaspoon dried thyme or dried oregano

finely grated rind of 1 lemon

¾ cup stale, coarse bread crumbs

3 tablespoons olive oil, plus extra for brushing

6–8 ripe black olives, pitted and sliced

2 tablespoons diced, drained vegetarian feta cheese (cut into ½-inch cubes)

salt and pepper

1. Preheat the broiler to medium. Put the onion, eggplant, mushrooms, and bell peppers on a large baking pan, placing the bell peppers cut side down. Brush with a little oil. Cook under the preheated broiler for 10–12 minutes, turning the onion, eggplant, and mushrooms halfway through, until beginning to blacken. Cut into even chunks.

2. Preheat the oven to 425°F. Place the broiled vegetables in a shallow ovenproof dish and arrange the tomatoes over them. Season with salt and pepper.

3. In a bowl, combine the garlic, parsley, rosemary, thyme, and lemon rind with the bread crumbs. Season with pepper. Add the oil to bind together the mixture. Spread the bread crumb mixture over the vegetables, followed by the olives and feta cheese.

4. Bake in the preheated oven for 10–15 minutes, or until the vegetables are heated all the way through and the topping is crisp. Serve immediately.

Spiced Vegetables

 SERVES 4   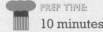 PREP TIME: 10 minutes    COOKING TIME: 30 minutes

nutritional information per serving	303 cal, 15g fat, 2.5g sat fat, 7g total sugars, 0.12g salt

If you've never tried okra before, this is a great recipe to start with. A sticky juice is released as it cooks, but it will gradually be absorbed as you stir the mixture.

INGREDIENTS

3 tablespoons ghee or vegetable oil

2 tablespoons slivered almonds

8 cardamom seeds

8 black peppercorns

2 teaspoons cumin seeds

1 cinnamon stick

2 fresh green chiles, seeded and chopped

1 teaspoon ginger paste

1 teaspoon chili powder

3 potatoes, cut into chunks

8 ounces okra, cut into 1-inch pieces

½ cauliflower, broken into florets

⅔ cup plain yogurt

⅔ cup vegetable stock or water

salt

freshly cooked rice, to serve

1. Heat 1 tablespoon of the ghee in a heavy saucepan. Add the almonds and cook over low heat, stirring continuously, for 2 minutes, or until golden.

2. Remove the almonds from the saucepan with a slotted spoon, drain on paper towels, and set aside. Place the cardamom seeds, peppercorns, cumin seeds, and cinnamon stick in a spice grinder or mortar and grind finely.

3. Add the remaining ghee to the saucepan and heat. Add the green chiles and cook, stirring frequently, for 2 minutes. Stir in the ginger paste, chili powder, and ground spices and cook, stirring continuously, for 2 minutes, or until they release their aroma.

4. Add the potatoes and season with salt. Cover and cook, stirring occasionally, for 8 minutes. Add the okra and cauliflower and cook for an additional 5 minutes.

5. Gradually stir in the yogurt and stock and bring to a boil. Cover and simmer for an additional 10 minutes, until all the vegetables are tender. Garnish with the reserved silvered almonds and serve with freshly cooked rice.

Red Curry with Mixed Greens

 SERVES 4

 PREP TIME: 10 minutes

COOKING TIME: 10 minutes

nutritional information per serving	304 cal, 25g fat, 16g sat fat, 6g total sugars, 0.5g salt

Have your rice cooked ready for serving because this fantastic, coconut milk-flavored, vegetable curry is quickly cooked in a wok.

INGREDIENTS

2 tablespoons peanut oil or vegetable oil

2 onions, thinly sliced

1 bunch of fine asparagus spears

1¾ cups coconut milk

2 tablespoons red curry paste

3 fresh kaffir lime leaves

1 (8-ounce) package baby spinach leaves

2 heads of bok choy, chopped

1 small head of Chinese cabbage, shredded

handful of cilantro, chopped

freshly cooked rice, to serve

1. Heat a wok over medium–high heat and add the oil. Add the onions and asparagus and stir-fry for 1–2 minutes.

2. Add the coconut milk, curry paste, and lime leaves and bring gently to a boil, stirring occasionally.

3. Add the spinach, bok choy, and Chinese cabbage, and cook, stirring, for 2–3 minutes, until wilted. Add the cilantro and stir well. Serve immediately with freshly cooked rice.

1

2

3

COOK'S NOTE
Remember to
check that fish
sauce is not an
ingredient in the
red curry paste
if you don't
include fish
in your diet.

Quinoa with Roasted Vegetables

 SERVES 2

PREP TIME: 10 minutes

COOKING TIME: 40–45 minutes

nutritional information per serving	418 cal, 23g fat, 2g sat fat, 14g total sugars, 0.1g salt

Quinoa (pronounced keen-wah) is an ancient grain originating from South America.

INGREDIENTS

2 bell peppers (any color), seeded and cut into chunky pieces

1 large zucchini, cut into chunks

1 small fennel bulb, cut into slim wedges

1 tablespoon olive oil

2 teaspoons very finely chopped fresh rosemary

1 teaspoon chopped fresh thyme

⅔ cup quinoa

1½ cups vegetable stock

2 garlic cloves, crushed

3 tablespoons chopped fresh flat leaf parsley

⅓ cup pine nuts, toasted

salt and pepper

1. Preheat the oven to 400°F. Place the bell peppers, zucchini, and fennel in a roasting pan large enough to hold the vegetables in a single layer.

2. Drizzle the olive oil over the vegetables and sprinkle with the rosemary and thyme. Season well with salt and pepper and mix well with clean hands. Roast for 25–30 minutes, until tender and lightly charred.

3. Meanwhile, place the quinoa, stock, and garlic in a saucepan. Bring to a boil, cover, and simmer for 12–15 minutes, until tender and most of the stock has been absorbed.

4. Remove the vegetables from the oven. Transfer the quinoa to the roasting pan. Add the parsley and pine nuts and toss together. Serve warm or cold.

SOMETHING
DIFFERENT
If you're unable
to buy highly
nutritious quinoa
(although it's
a very popular
grain these days)
use brown
long-grain rice
instead.

Stir-Fried Rice with Green Vegetables

PREP TIME:
5 minutes
plus cooling

COOKING TIME:
20–25 minutes

nutritional information per serving	288 cal, 7g fat, 0.8g sat fat, 3g total sugars, 0.2g salt

Thai basil should not be confused with sweet basil used in many Italian dishes. Thai basil has a slight licorice flavor that complements this dish perfectly.

INGREDIENTS

1¼ cups jasmine rice
2 tablespoons vegetable oil or peanut oil
1 tablespoon green curry paste
6 scallions, sliced
2 garlic cloves, crushed
1 zucchini, cut into thin sticks
1 cup trimmed green beans
10 asparagus spears, trimmed
3–4 fresh Thai basil leaves

1. Cook the rice in lightly salted, boiling water according to the package directions, drain well, cover, cool thoroughly, and chill.

2. Heat the oil in a wok and stir-fry the curry paste for 1 minute. Add the scallions and garlic and stir-fry for 1 minute.

3. Add the zucchini, beans, and asparagus and stir-fry for 3–4 minutes, until just tender. Break up the rice and add it to the wok. Cook, stirring continuously, for 2–3 minutes, until the rice is hot. Stir in the basil and serve immediately.

FREEZING TIP
Thai basil can be frozen in small quantities. Chop the leaves in a food processor, adding a little vegetable oil to coat. Pack into ice cube trays and freeze.

Bean Burgers

 SERVES 4   PREP TIME: 15 minutes   COOKING TIME: 20 minutes

nutritional information per serving	111 cal, 4g fat, 0.5g sat fat, 3.5g total sugars, 0.6g salt

Satisfy your appetite with these great-tasting homemade burgers that will taste far better than those you buy.

INGREDIENTS

1 tablespoon sunflower oil, plus extra for brushing

1 onion, finely chopped

1 garlic clove, finely chopped

1 teaspoon ground coriander

1 teaspoon ground cumin

2 cups finely chopped white button mushrooms

1 (15-ounce) can cranberry beans or red kidney beans, drained and rinsed

2 tablespoons chopped fresh flat-leaf parsley

all-purpose flour, for dusting

salt and pepper

hamburger buns and salad, to serve

1. Preheat the broiler to medium–high. Heat the oil in a heavy skillet over medium heat. Add the onion and cook, stirring frequently, for 5 minutes, or until softened. Add the garlic, coriander, and cumin and cook, stirring, for an additional minute. Add the mushrooms and cook, stirring frequently, for 4–5 minutes, until all the liquid has evaporated. Transfer to a bowl.

2. Put the beans in a small bowl and mash with a fork. Stir into the mushroom mixture with the parsley and season with salt and pepper.

3. Divide the mixture equally into four portions, dust lightly with flour, and shape into flat, round patties. Brush with oil and cook under the preheated broiler for 4–5 minutes on each side. Serve in hamburger buns with salad.

1

2

3

BE PREPARED

These will freeze well, so make a double batch. Open freeze on a sheet, then transfer to a plastic container. Freeze for up to three months. Cook from frozen.

Leek, Herb & Mushroom Risotto

 SERVES 8

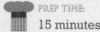 PREP TIME:
15 minutes

COOKING TIME:
30–35 minutes

nutritional information per serving	243 cal, 8.5g fat, 4g sat fat, 0.5g total sugars, 0.2g salt

A filling and comforting dish. Use a mixture of cultivated and wild mushrooms instead of cremini mushrooms, if you prefer.

INGREDIENTS

4¼ cups hot vegetable stock
2 tablespoons olive oil
1 small leek, coarsely chopped
3 garlic cloves, crushed
1 tablespoon fresh thyme
4 cups sliced cremini mushrooms
1½ cups risotto rice
¾ cup dry white wine
2 tablespoons butter
½ cup freshly grated vegetarian Parmesan-style cheese
2 tablespoons snipped fresh chives, plus extra to serve
salt and pepper
arugula and vegetarian Parmesan-style cheese shavings, to garnish

1. Keep the stock hot in a saucepan set over medium heat. Heat the oil in a separate saucepan over low heat. Add the leek, garlic, and thyme and cook for 5 minutes, until soft. Add the mushrooms and continue to cook for an additional 4 minutes, until soft.

2. Stir in the rice and cook stirring for 1 minute, then add the wine and heat rapidly until the liquid has almost completely evaporated.

3. Add a ladleful of stock and cook over medium heat, stirring, until it is absorbed by the rice. Continue adding the stock in the same way until it is all used up and the rice is creamy, plump, and tender.

4. If the risotto is a little undercooked, add a splash of water and continue cooking until creamy. Adding extra stock may make the risotto too salty.

5. Stir in the butter, followed by the cheese and chives. Season with salt and pepper. Serve in warm bowls topped with arugula, chives, and cheese shavings.

Ricotta, Spinach &
Pine Nut Pizza

 MAKES
1 pizza

PREP TIME:
20 minutes
plus rising

 COOKING TIME:
20–30 minutes

nutritional information per pizza	2601cal, 187g fat, 82g sat fat, 16g total sugars, 9.5g salt

Ricotta and fontina are two famous Italian cheeses and are the perfect combination for this great-tasting pizza.

INGREDIENTS

basic pizza dough

1½ cups white bread flour, plus extra for dusting

1 teaspoon active dry yeast

1 teaspoon salt

⅓ cup lukewarm water

1 tablespoon olive oil, plus extra for kneading

topping

1 (12-ounce) package fresh spinach

2 tablespoons olive oil, plus extra for brushing and drizzling

1 onion, thinly sliced

⅓ cup vegetarian ricotta cheese

½ teaspoon freshly grated nutmeg

2 tablespoons pine nuts

4 ounces vegetarian fontina cheese, sliced thinly

salt and pepper

1. Sift the flour into a mixing bowl and add the yeast and salt, making a small well in the center. Mix together the water and oil, add to the dry ingredients, and, using a rubber spatula, gradually combine all the ingredients to make a sticky dough.

2. Lightly flour the work surface and your hands and knead the dough for about 10 minutes, until it is smooth and elastic.

3. Cover the dough with some lightly oiled plastic wrap or a damp dish towel and let rise for about an hour, or until it has doubled in size.

4. Preheat the oven to 425°F. Brush a baking sheet with oil.

5. Roll out the dough on a lightly floured surface to a 10-inch circle. Place on the baking sheet and push up the edge a little. Cover and let stand in a warm place for 10 minutes.

6. Wash the spinach in cold water and dry well. Heat the oil in a saucepan, add the onion, and cook until soft and translucent. Add the spinach and cook, stirring, until just wilted. Remove the pan from the heat and drain off any liquid.

7. Spread the ricotta cheese evenly over the pizza crust, then cover with the spinach and onion mixture. Sprinkle over the nutmeg and pine nuts and season with salt and pepper. Top with the slices of fontina and drizzle with olive oil. Bake in the preheated oven for 20–30 minutes, until golden and sizzling. Serve immediately.

Smoky Mushroom & Herb Burgers

 SERVES 6   PREP TIME: 15 minutes   COOKING TIME: 10–15 minutes

nutritional information per serving	170 cal, 6g fat, 0.8g sat fat, 5g total sugars, 1.8g salt

Children will love helping mix and shape these vegan burgers.

INGREDIENTS

1 (15-ounce) can red kidney beans, rinsed and drained

2 tablespoons sunflower oil or vegetable oil, plus extra for brushing

1 onion, finely chopped

1⅔ cups finely chopped white button mushrooms

1 large carrot, shredded

2 teaspoons smoked paprika

¾ cup rolled oats

3 tablespoons dark soy sauce

2 tablespoons tomato paste

½ bunch of cilantro, including stems, chopped

3 tablespoons all-purpose flour

salt and pepper

to serve
soft rolls

salad greens

sliced avocado

tomato salsa or relish

1. Place the beans in a large bowl and mash as thoroughly as you can with a vegetable masher. Heat the oil in a skillet, add the onion, and sauté for 2 minutes, until translucent. Add the mushrooms, carrot, and paprika and sauté for an additional 4 minutes, until the vegetables are soft.

2. Add the sautéed vegetables to the beans with the oats, soy sauce, tomato paste, and cilantro. Season with salt and pepper and mix well. Divide into six equal portions and shape into patties, then turn in the flour to coat lightly.

3. Preheat a ridged grill pan until smoking. Lightly brush the tops of the patties with oil, then place oiled side down on the pan. Cook over medium heat for 2–3 minutes, until lightly charred underneath. Lightly brush the tops with oil, turn, and cook for an additional 2-3 minutes on the other side. Serve hot in soft rolls with salad greens, avocado slices, and salsa.

Mixed Nut Loaf

 **MAKES**
1 loaf

 **PREP TIME:**
15 minutes

COOKING TIME:
30-35 minutes

nutritional information per loaf	711 cal, 45g fat, 8.5g sat fat, 31g total sugars, 0.7g salt

Serve with roasted carrots, parsnips, and potatoes for an alternative Christmas feast.

INGREDIENTS

2 tablespoons butter, plus extra for greasing

2 garlic cloves, chopped

1 large onion, chopped

⅓ cup pine nuts, toasted

½ cup hazelnuts, toasted

½ cup walnuts, ground

⅓ cup cashew nuts, ground

2 cups fresh whole-wheat bread crumbs

1 egg, lightly beaten

2 tablespoons chopped fresh thyme, plus extra sprigs to garnish

1 cup vegetable stock

salt and pepper

cranberry & red wine sauce

1¾ cups fresh cranberries

½ cup sugar

1¼ cups red wine

1 cinnamon stick

1. Preheat the oven to 350°F. Grease a loaf pan and line it with wax paper. Melt the butter in a saucepan over medium heat. Add the garlic and onion and cook, stirring, for about 3 minutes. Remove the pan from the heat. Grind the pine nuts and hazelnuts. Stir all the nuts into the pan, add the bread crumbs, egg, thyme, and stock, and season with salt and pepper.

2. Spoon the mixture into the loaf pan and level the surface. Cook in the center of the preheated oven for 30 minutes, or until cooked all the way through and golden. The loaf is cooked when a toothpick inserted into the center comes out clean.

3. Halfway through the cooking time, make the cranberry and red wine sauce. Put all the ingredients in a saucepan and bring to a boil. Reduce the heat and simmer, stirring occasionally, for 15 minutes.

4. Remove the nut roast from the oven and invert. Garnish with sprigs of thyme and serve with the cranberry and red wine sauce.

Mushroom & Onion Quiche

 SERVES 4

 PREP TIME: 40 minutes plus chilling

COOKING TIME: 1¼ hours

nutritional information per serving	650 cal, 50g fat, 29g sat fat, 5g total sugars, 0.7g salt

Baking the empty dough shell first insures a crisp crust for this flavor-packed tart.

INGREDIENTS

pastry dough
1⅓ cups plus 1 tablespoon all-purpose flour, plus extra for dusting
pinch of salt
6 tablespoons butter, diced, plus extra for greasing
1 egg yolk
3 tablespoons ice-cold water

filling
4 tablespoons unsalted butter
3 red onions, halved and sliced
12 ounces mixed wild mushrooms, such as porcini, chanterelles, and morels
2 teaspoons chopped fresh thyme
1 egg
2 egg yolks
½ cup heavy cream
salt and pepper

1. Sift the flour with the salt into a bowl. Add the butter and rub into the flour with your fingertips until the mixture resembles fine bread crumbs. Beat the egg yolk with the water in a small bowl. Sprinkle the liquid over the flour mixture and combine with a rubber spatula to form a dough. Shape into a ball, wrap in aluminum foil, and chill in the refrigerator for 30 minutes.

2. Preheat the oven to 375°F. Lightly grease a 9-inch loose-bottom tart pan. Roll out the dough on a lightly floured surface and use to line the pan. Line the dough with parchment paper and fill with pie weights or dried beans. Bake in the preheated oven for 25 minutes. Remove the paper and weights and cool on a wire rack. Reduce the oven temperature to 350°F.

3. To make the filling, melt the butter in a large, heavy skillet over low heat. Add the onions, cover, and cook, stirring occasionally, for 20 minutes. Add the mushrooms and thyme and cook, stirring occasionally, for an additional 10 minutes. Spoon into the pastry shell and put the pan on a baking sheet.

4. Add the egg, egg yolks, and cream to a bowl, season with salt and pepper, and lightly beat together. Pour the egg mixture over the mushroom mixture. Bake in the oven for 20 minutes, or until the filling is set and golden. Serve hot or at room temperature.

Desserts

Baked Lemon Cheesecake

 SERVES 8   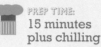 PREP TIME: 15 minutes plus chilling   COOKING TIME: 40–45 minutes

nutritional information per serving	316 cal, 17g fat, 10g sat fat, 22g total sugars, 0.5g salt

Try this lighter version of everyone's favorite cheesecake and then you won't feel so guilty having a second piece!

INGREDIENTS

4 tablespoons butter, plus extra for greasing

1½ cups crushed gingersnaps

3 lemons

1¼ cups vegetarian ricotta cheese

1 cup Greek-style yogurt

4 eggs

1 tablespoon cornstarch

½ cup granulated sugar

strips of lemon zest and confectioners' sugar, to decorate

1. Preheat the oven to 350°F. Grease an 8-inch round springform cake pan and line with parchment paper.

2. Melt the butter and stir in the cookie crumbs. Press into the bottom of the prepared cake pan. Chill until firm.

3. Meanwhile, finely grate the rind and squeeze the juice from the lemons. Add the ricotta, yogurt, eggs, cornstarch, and granulated sugar, and beat until a smooth batter is formed.

4. Carefully spoon the batter into the pan. Bake in the preheated oven for 40–45 minutes, or until just firm and golden brown.

5. Cool the cheesecake completely in the pan, then run a knife around the edge to loosen and slide onto a serving plate. Decorate with lemon zest and dust with confectioners' sugar.

GOES WELL WITH

A mixture of
fresh ripe berries
with a dash of
creme de cassis
or raspberry
liqueur.

Pecan Pie

 SERVES 8

 PREP TIME:
15 minutes
plus chilling

COOKING TIME:
50–55 minutes

nutritional information per serving	500 cal, 32g fat, 14g sat fat, 30g total sugars, 0.2g salt

This traditional pie is believed to have been created by the first French settlers in New Orleans.

INGREDIENTS

pastry dough
1⅔ cups all-purpose flour, plus extra for dusting
1 stick unsalted butter
2 tablespoons granulated sugar
a little cold water

filling
5 tablespoons unsalted butter
½ cup firmly packed light brown sugar
½ cup corn syrup
2 extra-large eggs, beaten
1 teaspoon vanilla extract
1 cup pecans

1. For the dough, place the flour in a bowl and rub in the butter with your fingertips until it resembles fine bread crumbs. Stir in the granulated sugar and add enough cold water to mix to a firm dough. Wrap in plastic wrap and chill for 15 minutes, until firm.

2. Meanwhile, preheat the oven to 400°F. Roll out the dough on a lightly floured surface and use to line a 9-inch loose-bottom, round tart pan. Prick the bottom of the dough with a fork. Chill for 15 minutes.

3. Place the tart pan on a baking sheet and line with parchment paper and pie weights or dried beans. Bake in the preheated oven for 10 minutes. Remove the paper and weights beans and bake for an additional 5 minutes. Reduce the oven temperature to 350°F.

4. For the filling, place the butter, brown sugar, and corn syrup in a saucepan and heat gently until melted. Remove from the heat and quickly beat in the eggs and vanilla extract. Coarsely chop the pecans and stir into the mixture. Pour into the pastry shell and bake for 35–40 minutes, until the filling is just set.

Amaretto Biscotti & Peaches

 SERVES 6

 PREP TIME:
20 minutes
plus cooling

 COOKING TIME:
40 minutes

nutritional information per serving	263 cal, 13g fat, 4g sat fat, 29g total sugars, 0.1g salt

Delicious crisp, almond-tasting cookies go perfectly with peaches and ice cream and are also great with an espresso coffee.

INGREDIENTS

1 egg white

½ cup superfine sugar

1 cup almond meal (ground almonds)

a few drops of almond extract

3 peaches or nectarines, sliced

2 tablespoons almond liqueur

1 pint vanilla ice cream (6 scoops)

1. Preheat the oven to 325°F. Line a baking sheet with parchment paper.

2. Place the egg white in a large bowl and beat until stiff. Gently fold the sugar, almond meal, and almond extract into the egg white with a large metal spoon until you have a smooth paste.

3. Roll teaspoonfuls of the mixture lightly between the palms of your hands to form 12 walnut-size balls. Place the balls ¾ inch apart on the prepared baking sheet. Bake in the preheated oven for about 20 minutes, until cracked and light golden. Remove the biscotti from the oven, and let cool, but keep the oven on.

4. Meanwhile, place the sliced peaches and 1 tablespoon of the almond liqueur in a heatproof dish. Cover and bake in the preheated oven for 20 minutes, until just tender. Remove from the oven, sprinkle with the remaining almond liqueur, and let cool.

5. Drain the peaches, reserving the juices, and arrange the peach slices in a fan on six side plates. Sandwich a scoop of ice cream between two biscotti and place on top of each peach fan. Spoon the reserved peach juices over the dessert and serve immediately.

Sweet Pumpkin Pie

 SERVES 8

 PREP TIME:
30 minutes
plus chilling

COOKING TIME:
50 minutes

nutritional information per serving	575 cal, 31g fat, 11g sat fat, 46g total sugars, 0.9g salt

With a nutty streusel topping, this is the pumpkin pie to beat them all. Serve with cream for a dessert to remember.

INGREDIENTS

1 cup plus 2 tablespoons all-purpose flour, plus extra for dusting

¼ teaspoon baking powder

1½ teaspoons ground cinnamon

¾ teaspoon ground nutmeg

¾ teaspoon ground cloves

1 teaspoon salt

¼ cup granulated sugar

4 tablespoons cold unsalted butter, diced, plus extra for greasing

3 eggs

1 (15-ounce) can pumpkin puree

1 (14-ounce) can condensed milk

½ teaspoon vanilla extract

1 tablespoon demerara sugar or other raw sugar

streusel topping

2 tablespoons all-purpose flour

¼ cup demerara sugar or other raw sugar

1 teaspoon ground cinnamon

2 tablespoons cold unsalted butter, diced

⅔ cup chopped pecans

⅔ cup chopped walnuts

1. Grease a 9-inch round pie plate. To make the pastry dough, sift the flour and baking powder into a large bowl. Stir in ½ teaspoon of the cinnamon, ¼ teaspoon of the nutmeg, ¼ teaspoon of the cloves, ½ teaspoon of the salt, and all the granulated sugar. Rub in the butter with your fingertips until the mixture resembles fine bread crumbs, then make a well in the center. Lightly beat one of the eggs and pour it into the well. Mix together with a wooden spoon, then shape the dough into a ball. Place the dough on a lightly floured surface, roll out, and use to line the prepared plate. Trim the edges, then cover and chill for 30 minutes.

2. Preheat the oven to 425°F. Put the pumpkin puree in a large bowl, then stir in the condensed milk and the remaining eggs. Add the remaining spices and salt, then stir in the vanilla extract and demerara sugar. Pour into the pastry shell and bake in the preheated oven for 15 minutes.

3. Meanwhile, make the topping. Mix the flour, demerara sugar, and cinnamon in a bowl, rub in the butter, then stir in the nuts. Remove the pie from the oven and reduce the heat to 350°F. Sprinkle the topping over the pie, then bake for an additional 35 minutes. Remove from the oven and serve hot or cold.

Key Lime Pie

 SERVES 8

 PREP TIME:
20 minutes
plus chilling

COOKING TIME:
20 minutes

nutritional information per serving	385 cal, 20g fat, 11g sat fat , 33g total sugars, 0.7g salt

This pie is from Florida, famous for its delicious tart limes.

INGREDIENTS

piecrust
25 graham crackers or gingersnaps (about 6 ounces)
2 tablespoons sugar
½ teaspoon ground cinnamon
5 tablespoons butter, melted, plus extra for greasing

filling
1 (14-ounce) can condensed milk
½ cup freshly squeezed lime juice
finely grated rind of 3 limes
4 egg yolks
whipped cream, to serve

1. Preheat the oven to 325°F. Grease a 9-inch round tart pan, about 1½ inches deep.

2. To make the piecrust, put the cookies, sugar, and cinnamon in a food processor and process until fine crumbs form—do not overprocess to a powder. Add the melted butter and process again until moistened.

3. Transfer the crumb mixture to the prepared tart pan and press evenly into the bottom and sides. Place the tart pan on a baking sheet and bake in the preheated oven for 5 minutes. Meanwhile, beat together the condensed milk, lime juice, lime rind, and egg yolks in a bowl until well blended.

4. Remove the tart pan from the oven, pour the filling into the piecrust, and spread out to the edges. Return to the oven for an additional 15 minutes, or until the filling is set around the edges but still wobbly in the center. Let cool completely on a wire rack, then cover and chill for at least 2 hours. Serve spread thickly with whipped cream.

3

3

4

SOMETHING DIFFERENT

If you don't have time to make the piecrust, bake the filling in a ready-to-bake piecrust.

Stuffed Baked Apples

 SERVES 4

PREP TIME:
10 minutes

COOKING TIME:
45 minutes

nutritional information per serving	241 cal, 5g fat, 0.5g sat fat, 35g total sugars, trace salt

There's nothing more comforting than a baked apple stuffed with apricots, ginger, and honey, and this recipe is the best.

INGREDIENTS

3 tablespoons blanched almonds

16 dried apricots

1 piece preserved ginger, drained

1 tablespoon honey

1 tablespoon syrup from the preserved ginger jar

¼ cup rolled oats

4 large Granny Smith apples

1. Preheat the oven to 350°F. Using a sharp knife, chop the almonds, apricots, and preserved ginger finely. Set aside until needed.

2. Place the honey and syrup in a saucepan and heat until the honey has melted. Stir in the oats and cook gently over low heat for 2 minutes. Remove the saucepan from the heat and stir in the almonds, apricots, and preserved ginger.

3. Core the apples, widen the tops slightly, and score horizontally around the circumference of each to prevent the skins from bursting during cooking. Place the apples in an ovenproof dish and fill the cavities with the stuffing. Pour just enough water into the dish to come about one-third of the way up the apples. Bake in the preheated oven for 40 minutes, or until tender. Serve immediately.

1

2

3

SOMETHING
DIFFERENT
For a change,
use dried cran-
berries or mixed
dried fruit
and pecans
or walnuts.

Broiled Pineapple with Nutty Yogurt

 SERVES 4

PREP TIME:
15 minutes

COOKING TIME:
5 minutes

nutritional information per serving	296 cal, 20.2g fat, 1.5g sat fat, 21g total sugars, trace salt

Not just for serving cold in a fruit salad, pineapple makes a quick and easy, warm dessert when grilled. Also try sprinkling the slices with cinnamon and brown sugar, wrapping in foil, and cooking on the barbecue.

INGREDIENTS

1 fresh pineapple
sunflower oil, for brushing
⅔ cup reduced-fat Greek-style yogurt
1 cup hazelnuts, skinned and coarsely chopped

1. Brush the broiler rack with oil and preheat the broiler to high. Cut off the leafy top from the pineapple and discard. Cut the pineapple into slices ¾ inch thick. Using a sharp knife, cut off the skin from each slice, then, holding the slices on their sides, cut out and discard the "eyes." Stamp out the core with an apple corer or cookie cutter and cut each slice in half.

2. Mix the yogurt and hazelnuts together in a bowl and set aside until needed.

3. Arrange the pineapple slices on the broiler rack and cook under the preheated broiler for 3–5 minutes, until golden. Serve with the nutty yogurt.

1

1

2

COOK'S TIP

Honey varies
widely in flavor;
the best quality,
with a distinctive
taste, is usually
made from a
single type
of blossom.

Baked Apricots with Honey

 SERVES 4　　 PREP TIME: 5 minutes　　 COOKING TIME: 12–15 minutes

nutritional information
per serving | 161 cal, 1.5g fat, 0.7g sat fat, 35g total sugars, trace salt

The season for fresh golden apricots is short, so take full advantage when you see them in the supermarket. This simple recipe really brings out their flavor.

INGREDIENTS

butter, for greasing
4 apricots, halved and pitted
¼ cup slivered almonds
¼ cup honey
pinch of ground ginger or grated nutmeg
vanilla ice cream, to serve (optional)

1. Preheat the oven to 400°F. Lightly grease an ovenproof dish large enough to hold the apricot halves in a single layer.

2. Arrange the apricot halves in the dish, cut sides up. Sprinkle with the almonds and drizzle the honey over the apricots. Dust with the ginger.

3. Bake in the preheated oven for 12–15 minutes, until the apricots are tender and the almonds golden. Remove from the oven and serve immediately, with ice cream on the side, if desired.

1

2

3

Prosecco Sorbet
with Grapes

 SERVES 4

PREP TIME:
10 minutes
plus freezing

COOKING TIME:
2–3 minutes

nutritional information per serving	213 cal, 0g fat, 0g sat fat, 42g total sugars, trace salt

A deliciously light and summery sorbet that's really easy to make.

INGREDIENTS

¾ cup superfine sugar

⅔ cup water

thinly pared strip of lemon zest

juice of 1 lemon

1½ cups prosecco

grapes and fresh mint sprigs, to decorate

1. Place the sugar and water in a saucepan with the lemon zest. Stir over low heat until the sugar dissolves, then boil for 2–3 minutes to reduce by half. Let cool and remove the lemon zest.

2. Combine the syrup with the lemon juice and prosecco, then churn the mixture in an ice cream maker following the manufacturer's instructions. Alternatively, pour into a freezerproof container and freeze, uncovered, beating at hourly intervals until frozen.

3. When ready to serve, let stand at room temperature to soften slightly, then scoop the sorbet into sundae glasses.

1

2

3

SOMETHING DIFFERENT
You could use an orange liqueur, such as Cointreau, in place of orange flower water.

Almond Meringues with Mixed Berries

 SERVES 6   PREP TIME: 20 minutes   COOKING TIME: 1–1¼ hours

nutritional information per serving	529 cal, 44g fat, 25g sat fat, 28g total sugars, 0.1g salt

This pretty meringue and cream dessert makes a change from pavlova and it's much easier to serve.

INGREDIENTS

2 extra-large egg whites

½ cup firmly packed light brown sugar

⅓ cup slivered almonds

2 cups heavy cream

2–3 tablespoons rose water, depending on strength, or 3 tablespoons dry white wine

1 tablespoon confectioners' sugar

4 cups prepared mixed berries, such as hulled and halved strawberries, pitted cherries, blueberries, raspberries, and blackberries

1. Preheat the oven to 250°F. Line two baking sheets with nonstick parchment paper. Place the egg whites in a large, grease-free bowl. Beat with an electric mixer until stiff, then beat in the brown sugar, 1 tablespoon at a time, beating well between each addition. The meringue should be glossy and holding soft peaks.

2. Spoon or pipe 18–20 golfball-size balls of meringue onto the baking sheets. Sprinkle generously with the slivered almonds and bake for 1–1¼ hours, until crisp. Let cool on a wire rack.

3. Place the cream, rose water, and confectioners' sugar in a large bowl and beat until the mixture just holds soft peaks. Layer the cooled meringues, spoonfuls of cream, and fruit in six tall glasses and serve immediately.

1

2

3

Sweet Peach Delight

 SERVES 4   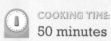 PREP TIME: 10 minutes   COOKING TIME: 50 minutes

nutritional information per serving	400 cal, 14g fat, 8g sat fat, 43g total sugars, 0.6g salt

If it's a quick to prepare, fruity dessert you want, this is just the one.

INGREDIENTS

4½ tablespoons butter
1 cup whole-wheat flour
1½ teaspoons baking powder
¾ cup low-fat or skim milk
½ cup sugar
4 large, ripe peaches, pitted, peeled, and sliced

1. Preheat the oven to 350°F. Melt the butter in a saucepan over low heat and pour it into the bottom of a shallow 8-inch square ovenproof dish.

2. Blend together the flour, baking powder, milk, and sugar and pour the mixture into the dish. Spoon the peach slices over the batter, but do not stir. Bake in the preheated oven for 50 minutes. Serve immediately.

1

2

2

COOK'S TIP
You can use
other seasonal
fruit for this
dish, such as
plums or pears.
You could also
use good-quality,
drained canned
fruits.

Strawberry & Cream Whoopie Pies

 MAKES 12   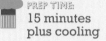 PREP TIME: 15 minutes plus cooling   COOKING TIME: 20–24 minutes

nutritional information per pie	363 cal, 22g fat, 14g sat fat, 23g total sugars, 0.6g salt

What's a Whoopie Pie? Well it's a mixture of a soft cookie, a cake, and a pie! Try this recipe and find out for yourself.

INGREDIENTS

2 cups all-purpose flour

1 teaspoon baking soda

large pinch of salt

1 stick butter, softened

¾ cup granulated sugar

1 extra-large egg, beaten

2 teaspoons rose water

⅔ cup buttermilk

confectioners' sugar, to dust

filling

1¼ cups heavy cream

¼ cup confectioners' sugar, sifted

3 tablespoons strawberry preserves

1½ cups sliced, hulled strawberries

1. Preheat the oven to 350°F. Line two to three large baking sheets with parchment paper. Sift together the all-purpose flour, baking soda, and salt.

2. Place the butter and sugar in a large bowl and beat with an electric mixer until pale and fluffy. Beat in the egg and rose water, followed by half the flour mixture and then the buttermilk. Stir in the rest of the flour mixture and mix until thoroughly incorporated.

3. Pipe or spoon 24 mounds of the mixture onto the prepared baking sheets, spaced well apart to allow for spreading. Bake in the preheated oven, one sheet at a time, for 10–12 minutes, until risen and just firm to the touch. Cool for 5 minutes, then using a spatula, transfer to a wire rack and let cool completely.

4. For the filling, place the cream in a bowl and whip until holding firm peaks. Fold in the sifted confectioners' sugar.

5. To assemble, spread the strawberry preserves on the flat side of half of the cakes, followed by the whipped cream and strawberries. Top with the rest of the cakes. Dust with confectioners' sugar.

Apple Pie Pizza

 MAKES
2 pizzas

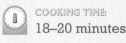 PREP TIME:
20 minutes
plus rising

COOKING TIME:
18–20 minutes

nutritional information per pizza	1,146 cal, 28g fat, 13g sat fat, 100g total sugars, 3.9g salt

If you can't imagine a sweet pizza, then try this and you'll be hooked.

INGREDIENTS

basic pizza dough
2¼ cups white bread flour, plus extra for dusting

1 teaspoon active dry yeast

1½ teaspoons salt

¾ cup lukewarm water

1 tablespoon olive oil, plus extra for kneading

topping
3 tablespoons butter

½ cup firmly packed light brown sugar

3 large apples, such as Pippin, peeled, cored, and thickly sliced

⅓ cup raisins

pinch of ground cloves

confectioners' sugar, for dusting

1. Sift the flour into a mixing bowl and add the yeast and salt, making a small well in the center. Mix together the water and oil and pour into the wet ingredients, and, using a rubber spatula, gradually combine all the ingredients to make a sticky dough.

2. Lightly flour the work surface and your hands and knead the dough for about 10 minutes, until it is smooth and elastic. Cover the dough with lightly oiled plastic wrap or a damp dish towel and let rise for about an hour, or until it has doubled in size.

3. Meanwhile, preheat the oven to 450°F. Punch down the dough to knock out the air, and gently knead for about a minute, then divide into two balls. To roll out the dough, flatten each ball, then, using a rolling pin, roll out on a lightly floured surface, giving a quarter turn between each roll.

4. Place the pizza crusts on two baking sheets, using a rolling pin to transfer them from the work surface.

5. Melt the butter in a heavy nonstick skillet over medium heat. Add the sugar, stirring well to dissolve. Let bubble for 5–6 minutes, until dark and syrupy. Add the apples, raisins, and cloves and cook for an additional 4–5 minutes, until the apples are starting to soften but are not completely cooked.

6. Using a slotted spoon, divide the apple mixture between the two pizza crusts. Spoon about half the syrup over the apple mixture, and reserve the remainder.

7. Bake in the preheated oven for 8–10 minutes, or until the crusts are crisp underneath. Drizzle with the reserved syrup, dust with confectioners' sugar, and serve warm.

Apple & Lime Sorbet

 SERVES 4

 PREP TIME:
15 minutes
plus freezing

COOKING TIME:
15–20 minutes

nutritional information per serving	227 cal, 0g fat, 0g sat fat, 56g total sugars, trace salt

An elegant dessert, yet economical, too, especially if you have an apple tree in the yard!

INGREDIENTS

3 crisp apples such as Granny Smith, Pippin, or Pink Lady, peeled, cored, and thinly sliced

2½ cups water, plus 3 tablespoons

1 cup sugar

finely grated zest and juice of 1 large lime

1 extra-large egg white, lightly beaten

¼ cup gin (optional)

slices of lime, to decorate

1. Place the apples and the 3 tablespoons of water in a saucepan. Cover and cook over low heat for 10–15 minutes, until tender. Let cool slightly. Transfer to a food processor and blend until completely smooth.

2. Place the sugar and remaining water in a clean saucepan and heat gently, stirring until the sugar has dissolved. Bring to a boil, then boil gently for 5 minutes. Remove from the heat. Stir in the apple and the lime zest and juice.

3. Let stand for about 1 hour, or until completely cool, then transfer to a freezerproof container, cover. and freeze for 2–3 hours, until frozen but still a little slushy in the middle.

4. Working quickly, break the frozen apple mixture into chunks and transfer to a food processor. Blend until smooth, then gradually add the egg white with the motor running. Continue blending for a few seconds until the sorbet looks pale and snowy. Return to the container and freeze for an additional 2–3 hours, until firm.

5. Serve scooped into chilled glasses, with a little gin poured over the top, if using, and decorate with slices of lime.

Breads & Baking

Garlic & Sage Bread

 MAKES
1 loaf

 PREP TIME:
20 minutes
plus rising

 COOKING TIME:
25–30 minutes

nutritional information per loaf	841 cal, 9g fat, 1g sat fat, 11g total sugars, 5g salt

The aroma of freshly baked bread, sage, and garlic is not to be missed. Don't let the bread cool unattended or you may find it gone!

INGREDIENTS

2 cups whole-wheat bread flour, plus extra for dusting

2¼ teaspoons active dry yeast

3 tablespoons chopped fresh sage, plus extra leaves, to garnish

1 teaspoon sea salt

3 garlic cloves, finely chopped

1 teaspoon honey

⅔ cup lukewarm water

vegetable oil, for brushing

vegetarian cream cheese, to serve

1. Sift the flour into a bowl and add the bran from the sifter. Stir in the yeast, sage, and salt. Set aside 1 teaspoon of the garlic and stir the remainder into the bowl. Make a well in the center and pour in the honey and water. Stir well until the dough begins to come together, then knead with your hands until it leaves the side of the bowl. Invert onto a lightly floured surface and knead for 10 minutes, or until smooth and elastic.

2. Brush a bowl with oil. Shape the dough into a ball, place it in the bowl, and place the bowl into a plastic bag or cover with a damp dish towel. Let rise in a warm place for 1 hour, or until the dough has doubled in volume.

3. Brush a baking sheet with oil. Invert the dough onto a lightly floured surface and knead for 2 minutes. Roll the dough into a long sausage, shape into a ring, and place it onto the baking sheet. Brush the outside of a bowl with oil and place it in the center of the ring to prevent it from closing up while the dough is rising. Place the baking sheet into a plastic bag or cover with a damp dish towel and let stand in a warm place for 30 minutes.

4. Preheat the oven to 400°F. Remove the bowl from the center of the loaf. Sprinkle the loaf with the reserved garlic and a little flour and bake in the preheated oven for 25–30 minutes, until golden brown and the loaf sounds hollow when tapped on the bottom with your knuckles. Transfer to a wire rack to cool. Cut into slices, spread with cream cheese, garnish with sage leaves, and serve.

3

4

Walnut & Seed Bread

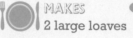

MAKES
2 large loaves

PREP TIME:
20 minutes
plus rising

COOKING TIME:
25–30 minutes

nutritional information per loaf	2,200 cal, 88g fat, 14.5g sat fat, 9g total sugars, 5.2g salt

A perfect loaf to serve with cheese. Freeze the second loaf if you don't need two.

INGREDIENTS

3¾ cups whole-wheat flour

3⅓ cups white bread flour, plus extra for dusting

2 tablespoons sesame seeds

2 tablespoons sunflower seeds

2 tablespoons poppy seeds

1 cup chopped walnuts

2 teaspoons salt

1½ tablespoons active dry yeast

2 tablespoons olive oil or walnut oil

3 cups lukewarm water

1 tablespoon melted butter or oil, for greasing

1. Mix together the flours, seeds, walnuts, salt, and yeast in a large bowl. Add the oil and water and stir well to form a soft dough. Invert the dough onto a lightly floured surface and knead well for 5–7 minutes, or until smooth and elastic.

2. Return the dough to the bowl, place the bowl in a plastic bag or cover with a damp dish towel, and let rise in a warm place for 1–1½ hours, or until the dough has doubled in size. Invert the dough onto a lightly floured surface and knead again for 1 minute.

3. Grease two 9-inch loaf pans well with melted butter. Divide the dough in half. Shape one piece the length of the pan and three times the width. Fold the dough in three lengthwise and place in one of the pans with the seam underneath. Repeat with the other piece of dough.

4. Cover and let rise again in a warm place for about 30 minutes, or until the dough is well risen above the pans.

5. Meanwhile, preheat the oven to 450°F. Bake in the center of the preheated oven for 25–30 minutes, until golden brown and the loaves sound hollow when tapped on the bottom with your knuckles. If the loaves are getting too brown during cooking, reduce the temperature to 425°F. Transfer to a wire rack to cool.

Pesto & Olive Soda Bread

 MAKES
1 loaf

 PREP TIME:
15 minutes

COOKING TIME:
30–35 minutes

nutritional information per loaf	2,156 cal, 43g fat, 4g sat fat, 21g total sugars, 6.7g salt

If you're not confident about baking with yeast, try this recipe—you're guaranteed to have great results. Use one of the pestos available in the supermarket or make your own. Either way, you will have a loaf to be proud of.

INGREDIENTS

olive oil, for greasing
2 cups all-purpose flour
2 cups whole-wheat flour
1 teaspoon baking soda
½ teaspoon salt
3 tablespoons pesto
about 1¼ cups buttermilk
½ cup coarsely chopped, pitted green olives,
milk, for glazing

1. Preheat the oven to 400°F and line and grease a baking sheet. Sift the flours, baking soda, and salt into a bowl, adding back any bran from the sifter.

2. Mix the pesto and buttermilk. Stir into the flour with the olives, mixing to a soft dough. Add more liquid, if needed.

3. Shape the dough into an 8-inch circle and place on the baking sheet. Flatten slightly and cut a deep cross with a sharp knife.

4. Brush with milk and bake in the preheated oven for 30–35 minutes, until golden brown. The loaf should sound hollow when tapped underneath. Transfer to a wire rack to cool.

1

2

3

COOK'S NOTE

Soda bread doesn't keep like yeast-risen recipes, so bake fresh on the day you want it.

Braided Poppy Seed Bread

 **MAKES**
1 loaf

 PREP TIME:
20 minutes
plus rising

COOKING TIME:
30–35 minutes

nutritional information per loaf	1,342 cal, 85g fat, 14g sat fat, 56g total sugars, 4.6g salt

For a change of pace, use other seeds, such as sesame, onion, or pumpkin, instead of poppy.

INGREDIENTS

1¾ cups white bread flour, plus extra for dusting

1 teaspoon salt

2 tablespoons instant skim milk powder

1½ tablespoons sugar

1 teaspoon active dry yeast

¾ cup lukewarm water

2 tablespoons vegetable oil, plus extra for greasing

⅓ cup poppy seeds

topping
1 egg yolk

1 tablespoon milk

1 tablespoon sugar

2 tablespoons poppy seeds

1. Sift the flour and salt together into a bowl and stir in the milk powder, sugar, and yeast. Make a well in the center, pour in the water and oil, and stir until the dough begins to come together. Add the poppy seeds and knead until completely combined and the dough leaves the side of the bowl. Invert onto a lightly floured surface and knead well for about 10 minutes, until smooth and elastic.

2. Brush a bowl with oil. Shape the dough into a ball, put it in the bowl, and place the bowl in a plastic bag or cover with a damp dish towel. Let rise in a warm place for 1 hour, or until doubled in volume.

3. Oil a baking sheet. Invert the dough onto a lightly floured surface and knead for 1–2 minutes. Divide into three equal pieces and shape each into a rope 10–12 inches long. Place the ropes side by side and press together at one end. Braid the dough, pinch the other end together, and tuck underneath.

4. Put the loaf on the prepared baking sheet, cover, and let rise in a warm place for 30 minutes. Meanwhile, preheat the oven to 400°F.

5. For the topping, beat the egg yolk with the milk and sugar. Brush the egg glaze over the top of the loaf and sprinkle with the poppy seeds. Bake in the preheated oven for 30–35 minutes, until golden brown. Transfer to a wire rack and Let cool.

Feta & Olive Biscuits

 MAKES
8 biscuits

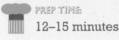 PREP TIME:
12–15 minutes

COOKING TIME:
12–15 minutes

nutritional information per biscuit	316 cal, 15g fat, 8g sat fat, 2g total sugars, 1.3g salt

These would be a hit for a brunch gathering arranged in a napkin-lined basket. Serve with unsalted butter, because the olives and cheese are already salty.

INGREDIENTS

3¼ cups all-purpose flour

5 teaspoons baking powder

¼ teaspoon salt

6 tablespoons butter, plus extra for greasing

⅓ cup chopped, pitted ripe black olives

⅓ cup chopped, drained sun-dried tomatoes in oil

½ cup crumbled, drained vegetarian feta cheese

1 cup whole milk, plus extra for glazing

pepper

1. Preheat the oven to 425°F. Grease a baking sheet.

2. Sift the flour, baking powder, and salt into a bowl, season with pepper, and rub in the butter evenly with your fingers.

3. Stir in the olives, tomatoes, and feta, then stir in just enough milk to make a soft, smooth dough.

4. Roll out on a floured surface to a 1¼-inch thick rectangle. Cut into 2½-inch squares. Place on the baking sheet, brush with milk, and bake in the preheated oven for 12–15 minutes, until golden.

5. Serve the biscuits fresh and warm, with extra butter, if needed.

2

3

4

BE PREPARED
Make the day before and, when cool, store in zip-topped bags. Reheat in a medium-high oven for 5-10 minutes before serving.

Cherry Tomato, Rosemary & Sea Salt Focaccia

 MAKES
1 loaf

 PREP TIME:
20 minutes
plus rising

COOKING TIME:
25–30 minutes

nutritional information per loaf	1,742 cal, 60g fat, 9g sat fat, 16g total sugars, 11g salt

A simplified version of the classic loaf studded with roasted cherry tomatoes and aromatic rosemary.

INGREDIENTS

⅓ cup olive oil

2 garlic cloves, crushed

2½ cups white bread flour, plus extra for kneading

2¼ teaspoons active dry yeast

2 teaspoons table salt

1 teaspoon sugar

1 cup lukewarm water

2 teaspoons finely chopped fresh rosemary

12–14 ripe red cherry tomatoes

¼ teaspoon flaky sea salt

1. Mix 2 tablespoons of the oil with all of the garlic. Set aside. Mix together the flour, yeast, table salt, and sugar in a large bowl. Add the remaining oil and water. Mix to a dough. Invert onto a lightly floured surface and knead for 10 minutes, until smooth and elastic, then knead in 1 tablespoon of the garlic-flavored oil.

2. Oil a rectangular baking pan measuring about 6½ x10 inches and at least 1½ inches deep. Press the dough over the bottom of the pan with your hands. Brush with the remaining garlic oil, then sprinkle with the rosemary. Cover loosely with plastic wrap and set aside in a warm place for about 1 hour, until puffed up and doubled in size.

3. Preheat the oven to 450°F. Place the tomatoes on the focaccia (squeeze in as many as you can) and press them into the dough. Sprinkle with the sea salt. Place in the preheated oven and immediately reduce the temperature to 400°F. Bake for 25–30 minutes, until golden brown and the center sounds hollow when tapped. Invert onto a wire rack to cool. Serve warm or cold.

1

2

3

COOK'S NOTE

If you don't have a deep baking pan, press out the dough to about the same size on an oiled baking sheet.

Date & Walnut Loaf

 **MAKES** 1 loaf   **PREP TIME:** 20 minutes   **COOKING TIME:** 35–40 minutes

nutritional information
per loaf

1,534 cal, 63g fat, 28g sat fat, 134g total sugars, 2.8g salt

This is a cross between cake and bread, so feel free to spread slices with butter, if you desire.

INGREDIENTS

¾ cup chopped, pitted dates

½ teaspoon baking soda

finely grated rind of ½ lemon

½ cup hot tea

3 tablespoons unsalted butter, plus extra for greasing

⅓ cup firmly packed light brown sugar

1 medium egg

1 cup all-purpose flour

1½ teaspoons baking powder

¼ cup chopped walnuts

walnut halves, to decorate

1. Preheat the oven to 350°F. Grease an 8½-inch loaf pan and line with parchment paper.

2. Place the dates, baking soda, and lemon rind in a bowl and add the hot tea. Let soak for 10 minutes, until softened.

3. Cream together the butter and sugar until light and fluffy, then beat in the egg. Stir in the date mixture.

4. Fold in the flour and baking powder, using a large metal spoon, then fold in the walnuts. Spoon the batter into the prepared cake pan and smooth the surface. Top with the walnut halves.

5. Bake in the preheated oven for 35–40 minutes, or until risen, firm, and golden brown. Cool for 10 minutes in the pan, then invert onto a wire rack to cool completely.

2

3

4

FREEZING TIP

Great for picnics and lunch boxes. You can wrap slices of the cooled loaf in plastic wrap and freeze for up to three months.

Banana & Coconut Loaf

 **MAKES**
1 loaf

 PREP TIME:
15 minutes

COOKING TIME:
1 hour

nutritional information per loaf	3,259 cal, 149g fat, 58g sat fat, 251g total sugars, 2.4g salt

Overripe bananas can be frozen unpeeled until you're ready to make this loaf.

INGREDIENTS

2 cups all-purpose flour

1½ teaspoons baking powder

1 cup sugar

¾ cup shredded dried coconut

2 eggs

⅓ cup sunflower oil, plus extra for greasing

2 ripe bananas, mashed

½ cup sour cream

1 teaspoon vanilla extract

shredded dried coconut, toasted, to decorate

1. Preheat the oven to 350°F. Grease and line a 1-quart loaf pan.

2. Sift together the flour and baking powder in a large bowl. Stir in the sugar and coconut. Beat together the eggs, oil, bananas, cream, and vanilla extract in a large bowl. Stir into the dry ingredients, mixing until evenly combined.

3. Spoon into the prepared pan, leveling with a rubber spatula. Bake in the preheated oven for about 1 hour, or until risen, firm, and golden brown.

4. Cool in the pan for 15 minutes, then invert onto a wire rack to cool completely. Decorate with shreds of coconut and serve.

Lemon Polenta Cake

 SERVES 8

 PREP TIME:
20 minutes
plus cooling

COOKING TIME:
30–35 minutes

nutritional information per serving	503 cal, 34g fat, 15g sat fat, 33g total sugars, 0.24g salt

Polenta is the Italian name for cornmeal and provides a nutty texture to a lemon syrup-soaked cake.

INGREDIENTS

1¾ sticks unsalted butter, plus extra for greasing

1 cup sugar

finely grated rind and juice of 1 large lemon

3 eggs, beaten

1½ cups almond meal (ground almonds)

⅔ cup instant polenta or cornmeal

1 teaspoon baking powder

crème fraîche or whipped cream, to serve

syrup

juice of 2 lemons

¼ cup sugar

2 tablespoons water

1. Preheat the oven to 350°F. Grease an 8-inch deep round cake pan and line with parchment paper.

2. Beat together the butter and sugar until pale and fluffy. Beat in the lemon rind, lemon juice, eggs, and almond meal. Sift in the polenta and baking powder and stir until evenly mixed. Spoon the batter into the prepared pan and smooth the surface. Bake in the preheated oven for 30–35 minutes, or until just firm to the touch and golden brown. Remove the cake from the oven and let cool in the pan for 20 minutes.

3. To make the syrup, place the lemon juice, sugar, and water in a small saucepan. Heat gently, stirring until the sugar has dissolved, then bring to a boil and simmer for 3–4 minutes, or until slightly reduced and syrupy. Invert the cake onto a wire rack, then brush half of the syrup evenly over the surface. Let cool completely.

4. Cut the cake into slices, drizzle the extra syrup over the top of the cake, and serve with crème fraîche.

SOMETHING
DIFFERENT
Use orange rind
and juice in place
of the lemon and
serve the cake as
a special dessert
accompanied by
caramel soaked
oranges.

Carrot Cake

 MAKES
6 bars

PREP TIME:
20 minutes
plus cooling

 COOKING TIME:
35-40 minutes

nutritional information per bar	493 cal, 24g fat, 8g sat fat, 54g total sugars, 0.6g salt

It's amazing that shredded carrot incorporated into a cake recipe can taste so delicious. Maybe it's the cream cheese frosting on the top!

INGREDIENTS

butter, for greasing
¾ cup all-purpose flour
1¼ teaspoons baking powder
pinch of salt
1 teaspoon ground allspice
½ teaspoon ground nutmeg
½ cup firmly packed light brown sugar
2 eggs, beaten
⅓ cup sunflower oil
2 carrots, shredded
1 banana, chopped
¼ cup chopped, toasted mixed nuts

frosting

3 tablespoons butter, softened
3 tablespoons vegetarian cream cheese
1⅓ cups confectioners' sugar, sifted
1 teaspoon fresh orange juice
grated rind of ½ orange
walnut halves or pieces, to decorate

1. Preheat the oven to 350°F. Grease a 7-inch square cake pan and line with parchment paper.

2. Sift the flour, baking powder, salt, allspice, and nutmeg into a bowl. Stir in the brown sugar, then stir in the eggs and oil. Add the carrots, banana, and nuts and mix well together.

3. Spoon the batter into the prepared pan and level the surface. Bake in the preheated oven for 35-40 minutes, or until golden and just firm to the touch. Let cool slightly. When cool enough to handle, invert onto a wire rack and let cool completely.

4. To make the frosting, put the butter, cream cheese, confectioners' sugar, and orange juice and rind in a bowl and beat together until creamy. Spread the frosting over the top of the cold cake, then use a fork to make shallow, wavy lines in the frosting. Decorate with the walnuts, cut the cake into bars, and serve.

Rich Chocolate Cake

 SERVES 12  PREP TIME: 20 minutes plus soaking   COOKING TIME: 40 minutes

nutritional information per serving	312 cal, 22g fat, 10g sat fat, 19g total sugars, 0.5g salt

A cake for adults who appreciate the intense flavor of a good-quality chocolate. No need for frosting—just a light sprinkling of confectioners' sugar. Enjoy.

INGREDIENTS

⅔ cup raisins

finely grated rind and juice of 1 orange

1½ sticks butter, diced, plus extra for greasing

3½ ounces bittersweet chocolate, at least 70 percent cocoa solids, broken into pieces

4 extra-large eggs, beaten

½ cup granulated sugar

1 teaspoon vanilla extract

½ cup all-purpose flour

½ cup almond meal (ground almonds)

½ teaspoon baking powder

pinch of salt

⅓ cup blanched almonds, lightly toasted and chopped

confectioners' sugar, sifted, to decorate

1. Preheat the oven to 350°F. Line a deep, loose-bottom, 10-inch round cake pan with wax paper. Grease the paper.

2. Put the raisins in a small bowl, add the orange juice, and let soak for 20 minutes.

3. Melt together the butter and chocolate in a small saucepan over medium heat, stirring. Remove from the heat and set aside to cool.

4. Using an electric mixer, beat together the eggs, sugar, and vanilla extract for 3 minutes, or until light and fluffy. Stir in the cooled chocolate mixture.

5. Drain the raisins if they have not absorbed all the orange juice. Sift the flour, almond meal, baking powder, and salt into the egg-and-sugar mixture. Add the raisins, orange rind, and almonds and fold together all of the ingredients.

6. Spoon into the cake pan and smooth the surface. Bake in the preheated oven for 40 minutes, or until a toothpick inserted into the center comes out clean and the cake starts to come away from the side of the pan. Let cool in the tin for 10 minutes, then remove from the pan, transfer to a wire rack, and let cool completely. Dust the surface with confectioners' sugar before serving.

Apple & Spice Cake

 SERVES 8   PREP TIME: 20 minutes   COOKING TIME: 50–60 minutes

nutritional information per serving	421 cal, 24g fat, 14g sat fat, 33g total sugars, 0.7g salt

This cake is wonderful served warm as a dessert or cooled and sliced for a coffee break.

INGREDIENTS

1½ sticks butter, softened, plus extra for greasing
1 cup sugar
finely grated zest of 1 lemon
2 extra-large eggs, beaten
1 cup plus 6 tablespoons flour
2 teaspoons baking powder
4 tablespoons milk

topping

¼ cup raw sugar
1 teaspoon ground cinnamon
¼ teaspoon ground cloves
2 crisp apples, such as Pink Lady
2 tablespoons cooled, melted butter
whipped cream or vanilla ice cream, to serve

1. Preheat the oven to 350°F. Lightly grease an 8-inch springform cake pan and line the bottom with nonstick parchment paper. Beat together the butter, sugar, and lemon zest until pale and creamy. Gradually add the eggs, beating well between each addition.

2. Fold in half the flour, baking powder, and milk, using a large metal spoon, then fold in the remainder until the batter is smooth. Spoon into the prepared pan and level the surface.

3. To make the topping, mix together the sugar, cinnamon, and cloves and sprinkle half the mixture over the top of the cake. Peel, core, and thinly slice the apples, then spread them evenly on top. Sprinkle with the remaining sugar mixture. Drizzle the melted butter over the cake.

4. Bake in the preheated oven for 50–60 minutes, until golden brown and the center is firm to the touch. Let stand for 10 minutes, then invert and remove the lining paper. Serve warm with whipped cream, or let cool and cut into slices.

1

2

3

SOMETHING
DIFFERENT
To vary, use
firm ripe
Bosc pears
instead of the
apples.

Espresso & Walnut Brownies

 MAKES 9   PREP TIME: 20 minutes plus cooling   COOKING TIME: 30 minutes

nutritional information per brownie	400 cal, 24g fat, 11g sat fat, 28g total sugars, 0.45g salt

Some people spend their whole life searching for the perfect brownie. You need go no farther.

INGREDIENTS

1 stick butter, plus extra for greasing

6 ounces semisweet chocolate, coarsely chopped

1⅓ cups plus 1 tablespoon all-purpose flour

2 teaspoons baking powder

2 tablespoons instant espresso coffee powder

⅔ cup chopped walnuts

2 eggs, beaten

⅔ cup firmly packed light brown sugar

1. Preheat the oven to 350°F. Grease and line a 7-inch square cake pan with parchment paper.

2. Put the butter and 2 ounces of the chocolate in a heatproof bowl. Place the bowl over a saucepan of simmering water and heat until the butter and chocolate have just melted. Remove from the heat and let cool for 10 minutes.

3. Mix together the flour, baking powder, coffee powder, remaining chocolate, and chopped walnuts in a large bowl. Place the eggs and sugar in another bowl and beat with a wooden spoon for a few minutes to break down any lumps of sugar. Add the cooled chocolate mixture, then the flour mixture, and beat until thoroughly combined.

4. Transfer the batter to the prepared pan and place in the center of the preheated oven. Bake for 30 minutes, until the brownie is set, crusted over, and cracked but still a little gooey in the center. Let cool in the pan before cutting into nine pieces and serving.

COOK'S NOTE
To prevent the
chocolate from
flying about when
you chop it, have
a bowl of hot
water and a clean
cloth on hand.
Warm the knife
in the water,
wipe dry, and
the job will be
a lot easier.

Oat Bars

MAKES 16   PREP TIME: 10 minutes   20 minutes

nutritional information per bar	250 cal, 16g fat, 7g sat fat, 13g total sugars, trace salt

Going on a long journey? You'll be really pleased you took a batch of these with you to keep you going, and so will everyone else you meet.

INGREDIENTS

1½ sticks unsalted butter, plus extra for greasing

3 tablespoons honey

¾ cup demerara sugar or other raw sugar

⅓ cup smooth peanut butter

2½ cups rolled oats

⅓ cup chopped dried apricots

2 tablespoons sunflower seeds

2 tablespoons sesame seeds

1. Preheat the oven to 350°F. Grease and line an 8-inch square baking pan.

2. Melt the butter, honey, and sugar in a saucepan over low heat. When the sugar has melted, add the peanut butter and stir until everything is well combined. Add all the remaining ingredients and mix well.

3. Press the mixture into the prepared pan and bake in the preheated oven for 20 minutes. Remove from the oven and let cool in the pan, then cut into 16 squares and serve.

COOK'S NOTE

Use nonstick parchment paper to line your pan; it's easier to do than with wax paper.

Blueberry Granola Bars

 MAKES 12   PREP TIME: 10 minutes   COOKING TIME: 20 minutes

nutritional information per bar	270 cal, 15g fat, 6g sat fat, 11g total sugars, 0.2g salt

Great for lunch boxes, these will keep for up to a week in an airtight container—if they last that long!

INGREDIENTS

1 cup dried blueberries
2½ cups rolled oats
3 tablespoons light brown sugar
½ cup chopped pecans
3 tablespoons sunflower seeds
1 tablespoon sesame seeds
¼ teaspoon ground cinnamon
½ cup light corn syrup
1 stick butter, plus extra for greasing

1. Preheat the oven to 350°F. Grease and line a 7 x 11-inch baking pan.

2. Put the blueberries, oats, sugar, pecans, seeds, and cinnamon into a large bowl.

3. Heat the corn syrup and butter in a saucepan over low heat until just melted. Stir in the dry ingredients to coat thoroughly. Transfer the batter to the prepared pan and smooth the surface.

4. Place in the preheated oven and bake for 20 minutes, until golden. Remove from the oven and let cool for 5 minutes before marking into 12 bars.

5. Let cool completely in the pan, then cut through the markings to create 12 bars.

Low-Fat Banana & Date Muffins

 MAKES 12   PREP TIME: 15 minutes   COOKING TIME: 20–25 minutes

nutritional information per muffin : 142 cal, 0.7g fat, 0.3g sat fat, 18g total sugars, 0.3g salt

Adding banana to this low-fat recipe is the secret to creating a moist muffin.

INGREDIENTS

oil or melted butter, for greasing (if using)

1¾ cups all-purpose flour

2 teaspoons baking powder

¼ teaspoon salt

½ teaspoon ground allspice

⅓ cup sugar

2 egg whites

2 ripe bananas, sliced

½ cup chopped, pitted dried dates

¼ cup skim milk

⅓ cup maple syrup

1. Preheat the oven to 400°F. Grease a 12-cup muffin pan or line with 12 muffin cups.

2. Sift together the flour, baking powder, salt, and allspice into a large bowl. Add the sugar and mix together.

3. In a separate large bowl, beat the egg whites. Mash the bananas in another bowl, then add them to the egg whites. Add the dates, pour in the milk and maple syrup, then stir together gently to mix. Make a well in the center of the dry ingredients and pour in the liquid ingredients. Stir gently until just combined; do not overmix.

4. Spoon the batter into the prepared muffin pan. Bake in the preheated oven for 20–25 minutes, until well risen, golden brown, and firm to the touch.

5. Let the muffins cool in the pan for 5 minutes, then serve warm or transfer to a wire rack and let cool completely.

3

3

4

FREEZING TIP

All muffins freeze well. Once cooked, pack into zip-topped bags and freeze for up to three months. Thaw them as needed before warming in the microwave for 30–40 seconds.

Nectarine & Banana Muffins

MAKES 12

PREP TIME:
15 minutes

COOKING TIME:
20 minutes

nutritional information
per muffin

212 cal, 9g fat, 1.5g sat fat, 12g total sugars, 0.4g salt

The combination of nectarine and banana is delicious, and this recipe will become a favorite.

INGREDIENTS

oil or melted butter,
for greasing (if using)

2 cups all-purpose flour

1 teaspoon baking soda

¼ teaspoon salt

¼ teaspoon ground allspice

½ cup sugar

½ cup chopped almonds

1 large ripe nectarine,
peeled, pitted, and chopped

1 ripe banana, sliced

2 extra-large eggs

⅓ cup sunflower oil or peanut oil

⅓ cup thick plain yogurt or
banana-flavored yogurt

1 teaspoon almond extract

1. Preheat the oven to 400°F. Grease a 12-cup muffin pan or line with 12 muffin cups. Sift together the flour, baking soda, salt, and allspice into a large bowl. Stir in the sugar and almonds.

2. In a separate large bowl, mash the nectarine and banana, then beat in the eggs, oil, yogurt, and almond extract. Make a well in the center of the dry ingredients and pour in the beaten liquid ingredients. Stir gently until just combined; do not overmix.

3. Spoon the batter into the prepared muffin pan. Bake in the preheated oven for 20 minutes, until well risen, golden brown, and firm to the touch.

4. Let the muffins cool in the pan for 5 minutes, then serve warm or transfer to a wire rack and let cool completely.